HARD WIRED

PRAISE FOR
HARD WIRED

———

"Hard Wired provides a roadmap and actionable steps to train your mind for peak performance, and it is especially needed when so many experience mental fog and distraction. As elite athletes have paved the way for physical fitness, Brandon harnesses learnings from esports and the latest research to pave the way for cognitive fitness."

— TODD HARRIS, COFOUNDER OF HI-REZ
STUDIOS, FOUNDER OF SKILLSHOT MEDIA

"If you're looking for a personal trainer for your mind, then look no further. Brandon's World's Toughest Mudder experience will leave you inspired and ready to put into action all

the lessons he shares on how to train your mind to achieve success. A must-read!"

— RICH KELLER, CHIEF EMPOWERMENT OFFICER - SCORE

"This book is a great insight into how to improve your mind and push your limits. With personal stories, scientific evidence, and practical applications - this book offers a roadmap to help any reader in reaching their goals, no matter how crazy they may seem."

— JAKE MIDDLETON, FOUNDER OF ESPORTS TRAINER, LLC

"For those looking to maximize their potential, Hard Wired is a must. Brandon shows how we can implement small changes that yield big results."

— DYLAN GAMBARDELLA, CO-FOUNDER OF NEXT GEN

"Brandon reminds us that there is more to training than just physical exertion and repetition. Each and every performance contains a vast mental aspect that many neglect to train. His insight into what it takes to become an elite performer will impact anyone looking to succeed at their domain."

— DAN HIMMELSTEIN, ESPORTS PERFORMANCE COACH
& FOUNDER OF PREMIER ESPORTS ACADEMY

"*Brandon's down-to-earth approach to training the mind makes this important information accessible to everyone.*"

"*Fascinating deep dive into the mind and it's complex relationship with performance. Loving that esports athletes are finally getting the validation they deserve!*"

"*Brandon traverses the new world of Esports and bridges the gap between traditional sports seamlessly. If you're looking to train your mind and improve your gameplay, Hard Wired will be a great resource.*"

"*Hard Wired will make you rethink your limits and inspire you to think about how your mind is your greatest superpower. Beautifully written with anecdotes, scientific evidence, and snippets of his life story, Brandon Gustafson's Hard Wired is a great read for anyone interested in training their mind* "

"*Hard Wired is a must read! Brandon effectively shares personal stories and powerful insights that can connect with any reader.*"

—MIRACLE OLATUNJI, AUTHOR OF PURPOSE
AND DIRECTOR OF INNOVATION AT THRIVE

"*Hard Wired is a great reminder that anything is possible if you believe in the power of your mind.*"

— JILLIAN RICHARDSON, AUTHOR OF UNLONELY PLANET

"*One of the only books I've read that consistently focuses on the realistic challenges behind self-improvement. Instead of blasting you with complicated jargon, Gustafson focuses on making sure that the information is easy to understand and implement. Fantastic read!*"

— DEREK KONTNY, AUTHOR OF VACANT SKIES

HARD WIRED

A PRACTICAL GUIDE TO
TRAINING YOUR MIND

BRANDON GUSTAFSON

This book contains advice and information relating to health care. It should be used to supplement rather than replace the advice or your doctor or another trained health professional. If you know or suspect you have a health problem, it is recommended that you seek your physician's advice before embarking on any medical program or treatment. All efforts have been made to assure the accuracy of the information contained in this book as of the date of publication. This publisher and the author disclaim liability for any medical outcomes that may occur as a result of applying the methods suggested in this book.

NEW DEGREE PRESS

HARD WIRED
A Practical Guide to Training Your Mind

ISBN 978-1-64137-256-5 *Paperback*
      978-1-64137-257-2 *Ebook*

While the author has made every effort to provide accurate Internet addresses at the time of publication, neither the publisher nor the author assumes any responsibility for errors, or for changes that occur after publication. Further, the publisher does not have any control over and does not assume any responsibility for author or third-party websites or their content.

Cover Design: Srdjan Filipovic
Author Photo: Rose Mary Lambert

To anyone who has ever struggled to believe in themselves. You have greatness within you.

CONTENTS

INTRODUCTION
THE RACE THAT
REWIRED MY MIND

———

"What color is grass?"

"Green..."

"What kind of animal is Disney's Mickey?"

"A mouse..."

Whew, passed!

It was 3 a.m. in the desert on the outskirts of Las Vegas and medics were checking on me to make sure I was okay to keep going. I could barely answer over my chattering teeth. I swore that hypothermia had to be setting in.

After what felt like an eternity, the medics took one more look at my disheveled body and waved me through. I had just run 45 miles in the World's Toughest Mudder and I had nine more hours between me and the finish line. I could barely walk, it felt like I dislocated my shoulder, and the buzz from electric shocks reverberated throughout my body. How was I supposed to survive another 9 hours?

***

Never underestimate the power of YouTube's suggested videos. One suggestion changed my entire life.

A 2015 highlight video for the World's Toughest Mudder, a 24-hour obstacle race, popped up and I was intrigued. The video started: "Life at its best is in the moment. You're not thinking about the future. You're not thinking about the past. But everything you've ever done in your life, you're using right then."

I wanted to experience that feeling.

The video showed the race happening in the desert outside of Las Vegas with scorching sun during the day and frigid air at night. I saw 1,000 crazy people and their support crews excited to run for 24 hours...

The race was a 5-mile loop with around 20 obstacles in each lap. The goal was to complete as many laps as possible in 24 hours. There was a pit area, as they have in NASCAR races, at the end of the loop where runners could stop for food, supplies, and words of encouragement. Obstacles included crawling through mud under barbed wire, running up slick quarter pipes, monkey bars over water, cargo nets, a 35-foot cliff jump, and a challenge like the board game operation, it will shock you if the metal pole you're using to retrieve a wristband touches the edge of a circle cutout. With all the water on the course, runners wore wetsuits just to stay warm.

One of the runners said, "This is hands down, the most amazing group of human beings you'll ever find in the world."

The video showed people from all walks of life taking on this epic challenge, helping each other out along the way.

Completing that race would be awesome, I thought to myself.

The only problem?

I had never run more than a 5k in my life.

It made me wonder if I could do it.

∗∗∗

I was a shy, quiet kid in high school. I never smiled showing my teeth. I liked to stay home and play video games, and I often doubted myself.

As a sophomore in high school, my friend Ben finally persuaded me to go to the local gym after months of me finding excuses not to go.

I had no idea what I was doing.

I couldn't do a push-up.

I felt self-conscious about being there.

Despite my protests, Ben had me trying all sorts of exercises. They were so challenging my arms shook awkwardly. I made it through the hour-long workout and I had the strangest feeling. I felt confident — something I'd rarely felt before.

All of a sudden, I believed in myself. I felt strong and capable of anything.

In that single hour, I didn't gain any muscle, I didn't change my body composition, and I didn't have a six-pack, but I did change my mind.

I never wanted that feeling to go away. That fateful day my sophomore year would change the trajectory of my life.

There I was, just five years later, on a plane destined for Las Vegas and the World's Toughest Mudder.

Ultramarathons, triathlons, and ninja warrior courses are all challenging, but not quite like World's Toughest Mudder. I would be running on uneven rocky terrain, jumping in freezing water, climbing over obstacles, and pushing my muscles and mind to the limit for 24-hours straight. This was the most epic obstacle course race in the world.

And I was about to take it on.

***

Before heading out I checked to make sure I had everything I would need.

Wetsuit and headlamp? Check.

Six pairs of socks? Buff? CamelBak? Check, check, check.

Pickle juice, beef sticks, and Red Bull? Check.

Okay, ready to go. My crew and I hauled everything to our campsite in the pit and settled in. The atmosphere was electric, pit crews were running around making sure everything was in order before the chaos that was about to ensue.

I ducked into my tent to get some shade from the hot desert sun, grabbed *The Obstacle Is the Way* by Ryan Holiday, and read a bit before the event started. I knew that the next 24-hours would be grueling, so I wanted to make sure I was in the right state of mind.

At 30 minutes before go-time, I gathered near the starting gates with all the other runners for the final debrief. I triple checked my gear, smiled for pre-race photos, and got settled. As I knelt down, I could feel the sweat already dripping down my back from the hot desert sun. I tried to slow my racing mind as I stared out at the rugged course that would be my home for the next 24 hours. Would I be strong enough to take on this colossal mental and physical challenge? My mind answered back; yes.

I looked up and heard Tough Mudder MC Sean Corvelle say, "We are people that have something inside of us that cannot be denied... The only way you can fail is if you did not find your best." I was about to discover what my best really was.

The countdown began and when the clock struck 12 and the horn blared, we were off. The stampede of runners charged up the hill towards a towering cargo net climb, leaving behind a wall of dust.

The race was on.

**

The first 20 miles went as smoothly as I could've hoped. I'd successfully completed most of the obstacles and was making good time. Anytime I failed an obstacle, I had to run an extra penalty loop. Failing every obstacle would extend the 5-mile lap to over 6 miles, not something I wanted to experience.

Each lap I would stop in the pit, eat a peanut butter sandwich, and drink some Gatorade. Without my crew, consisting of my good friend Cole and my parents, I would have been in a world of hurt.

The sun was setting and I knew the temperature was about to start dropping. I felt like I could squeeze in one more lap before having to put on my wetsuit —, which would make it harder to run. I hurried through the lap, racing the sunset, just trying to stay warm until I could get back to the pit. I made it back just as I felt goose bumps forming on my arms and quickly put on my wetsuit, thankful for some warmth.

It was dark out, so I had to put on my headlamp and attach a flashing strobe to my racing bib. I looked like I was ready to go surfing, not crawling through the mud.

With the wetsuit restricting my movements my pace slowed by a couple minutes per mile, but I felt strong and continued to make good progress. After 35 miles, I still felt good. I had just downed my seventh PB sandwich, took a big swig of pickle juice to prevent cramps, had a couple bites of a beef stick, and pounded as much Red Bull as my stomach could handle. I felt good about my race and getting to 75 miles, but a race like this has a funny way of smacking you in the face.

Those crazy race organizers decided to open up The Cliff, a terrifying 35 foot jump into pitch-black freezing water, at midnight. Why not?

As I neared the end of my eighth lap, I approached The Cliff, the final obstacle standing before me and the pit. Despite my fear of heights, I had jumped off boats into water so I thought, "How bad could this be?"

I jumped off the platform and plummeted like a cannonball towards the water, bracing for impact. I wasn't ready for it though. I hadn't anticipated the impact of entering the water would be so strong it would force my eyes open and wash away my contacts.

For some this may be no big deal, but without my contacts, I am legally blind. I can still see, but nothing has edges. I flopped like a fish out of water, trying to get to shore and the pit.

I climbed up the cargo net and out onto the track, but couldn't see the path forward. I stumbled around until two other runners saw me struggling. They took me around their arms and guided me back to the pit and my crew. Cole helped me the rest of the way to our tent. Then we scavenged around my bag, praying there would be more contacts. In a random side pocket, there was an old box of contacts that had probably been hidden in there for over a year. There were only two contacts left.

I sprayed water on my hands and with muddy fingers put in the replacement contacts. I don't know what I would have done without them. I felt so stupid for not bringing more.

This is where things started to unravel.

The constant barrage of water obstacles had my headlamp on the fritz. It would go in and out for the next two hours, leaving me running in pure darkness at times. I am not sure where it came from, but this frustration and anger started bubbling up. Maybe because I was running in pure darkness, but I decided to embrace the dark side and use that anger as fuel. I was tired and pissed off. I needed to grab hold of whatever motivation I could find, and anger seemed like as good a source as any. It was not pretty, but I completed lap nine around 3 a.m.

I got back to the pit in a state of despair. Despite wearing a wetsuit, I was shivering uncontrollably and my entire body felt numb. Cole got me some hot soup, fixed my headlamp, and got my wetsuit ready to go. I was 45 miles in and could barely move my legs.

Yet, I trudged on to the start. After nightfall, there are medics at the start who ask questions to make sure you are okay to keep going.

As I trudged to the starting line, I met my 3 a.m. medic.

I wasn't running anymore. The muscles in my legs started to fail me and it took all I had just to lift them. I was falling asleep on my feet and my shoulders throbbed despite all the ibuprofen I was taking. It might have been a slow lap, but I finished lap 10 and reached the 50-mile mark.

At this point, my mind was fried and it took all I had just to keep putting one foot in front of the other. I continued moving forward in the darkness, getting colder with each passing mile. Then I noticed something strange. The sky began to change.

The black sky turned to dark blue and I could catch a glimmer of orange light. For the first time that night I felt hope. I was almost there. As the giant red-orange ball peaked over the horizon, a sense of relief washed over me. I don't think I have ever been so happy to see a sunrise in my life. I finished lap 11 and went out for my final lap.

That final lap was a blur, but I remember climbing down the final obstacle and swimming the last section of the course. As I climbed out of the water and ran toward the finish line, I thought back to all the people who pushed me, the hours of work I'd put in, and the sacrifices I'd made to get to that point.

I thought back to the YouTube video, "Life at its best is in the moment." I was living in the moment. I had just completed 60 miles in 24 hours and found what I was looking for.

**

My year of preparation for the World's Toughest Mudder taught me a valuable lesson. We are all capable of rewiring our minds and getting to the place we want to go if we take the time to work on our minds. Everything I worked on to prepare for this race helped me build the mind I needed to complete this challenge. Through training, I hard wired my mind.

I learned everything I possibly could about running and nutrition. I made sure I was taking care of my physical health. I worked on my mindset to develop confidence. I did hard things every day in order to build up my mental toughness. I found strategies to help me manage my emotions. I practiced making decisions that I knew I would face out on the course so I would be prepared. I discovered the flow state and how to tap into it.

Training for and completing the World's Toughest Mudder convinced me that our mind is our greatest superpower. I discovered that our mind has the power to help us achieve our biggest goals if we train it to do so.

In this book, we'll unpack the science of rewiring our minds and discover what it takes to train your mind to become hard wired. Ready! Set! Go!

1

INSIDE THE MIND

———

"You are today where your thoughts have brought you; you will be tomorrow where your thoughts take you."

— JAMES ALLEN

"Oh, I could never do that. I'm not tough enough."

I was having coffee with my friend and had just finishing explaining how I completed the World's Toughest Mudder. His response after the story was one I'd heard nearly every time.

Why was I tough enough? I wasn't special. I didn't grow up with any particular advantages. But I'd figured it out.

Then a thought hit me.

What if you could have a personal trainer for your mind?

***

"Our culture has become hooked on the quick-fix, the life hack, efficiency. Everyone is on the hunt for that simple action algorithm that nets maximum profit with the least amount of effort. There's no denying this attitude may get you some of the trappings of success, if you're lucky, but it will not lead to a calloused mind or self-mastery. If you want to master the mind and remove your governor, you'll have to become addicted to hard work. Because passion and obsession, even talent, are only useful tools if you have the work ethic to back them up."

— DAVID GOGGINS, CAN'T HURT ME: MASTER
YOUR MIND AND DEFY THE ODDS

David Goggins, a Navy Seal, ultra-marathoner, and author of *Can't Hurt Me* has been called the toughest man on the planet. He is the master of using pain and suffering to build an unstoppable mindset. Goggins weighed nearly 300 pounds and realized his life was too comfortable. He decided to make a change and challenged himself to build his mental toughness and set out to become a Navy Seal.

Goggins was over the age limit for BUD/S (Seal Training), but there was a program that enabled enlisted men to enter training after the cutoff. Only problem was the program was ending in 3 months and Goggins had to lose over 100 pounds. Impossible? Not for Goggins.

After losing the weight, Goggins still had to pass BUD/S. It took three attempts, but he made it and was assigned to SEAL Team 5.

After several of his friends died in a helicopter crash in Afghanistan in 2005, Goggins decided to take on ultra-running in an effort to raise money for the Lone Survivor Foundation. He searched for the most challenging races in the world and found the Badwater 135, a grueling race through California's Death Valley in the heat of summer.

However, runners had to complete 100 miles in 24 hours in another race in order to qualify. After finding out about this rule, Goggins signed up for a 24 hour race in San Diego taking place just four days later.

Without any prior training and only some Myoplex protein drinks and Ritz crackers for nutrition, Goggins had to run around a one mile track 100 times to be considered for the Badwater.

Goggins started the race too fast and by mile 70, he was hurting. Goggins had shin splints, broken both his feet, and could not even stand up to make it to the bathroom. He had to find a way to run 30 more miles, despite his body being physically destroyed. He realized he had to break it down into manageable chunks and find a way to keep going.

Goggins hydrated himself and found the strength to stand back up and keep going. Around 81 miles in he was running at such a slow pace that his crew member told him he was not going to have enough time to finish the 100 miles unless he picked up the pace.

"This is when I realized that the human mind, once everything gets connected, once the mind knows you're not going to quit something, it's going to try to find more. It's going to try to give you more. Once it realizes you're not going to take the path of least resistance – you're going to stay here until it's done – my mind and my body and my spirit became one for the first time ever," explained Goggins.

Goggins found another level. He completed 101 miles, one extra just to be sure, in just under 19 hours. Through physical suffering and tremendous challenge, he discovered how powerful his mind truly was.

"Mental toughness is constantly facing the things you don't want to face," explained Goggins. This is the simple secret to strengthening our mind. Every time we face resistance and push past it, we come out stronger on the other side.

This begs the question, is Goggins' mindset teachable?

***

Carol Dweck Ph. D., a researcher at Stanford and author of *Mindset*, is convinced it is.

Fascinated with learning how people cope with failures, she began researching students to observe how they reacted to challenging situations. Some students became discouraged when faced with adversity. Through her research, she discovered "the views you adopt for yourself profoundly affect the way you lead your life."

The students who struggled when faced with a challenge carried with them a belief their abilities are fixed at birth – dubbed a *fixed mindset*. When we have a fixed mindset, we believe our traits, abilities, intelligence, and moral character are immutable. With this mindset, we feel the need to continually prove ourselves, to show how smart we are because our self-perception is wrapped up in proving to the world we are intelligent.

"The passion for stretching yourself and sticking to it, even (or especially) when it's not going well, is the hallmark of the growth mindset," Dweck explained.

While some of the students despaired when challenged, others rose to the occasion. They chose to adopt a different mindset, a *growth mindset*, whether they realized it or not.

The core idea behind the growth mindset is that belief that our skills and abilities are not fixed; they are something that can be developed. Our potential is not limited, simply unknown. With a growth mindset it doesn't matter where we are today, what matters is that we are capable of growing and expanding our minds.

We have the ability to change our inner monologue from "I can't" and "I'm a failure" to "What can I learn from this and how can I get better?"

The growth mindset sounds like a great idea, but Dweck wanted to know if it would translate into the real world. She asked the question, "If we gave students a growth mindset, if we taught them how to think about their intelligence, would that benefit their grades?"

Dweck and her colleagues took around 100 seventh graders performing poorly in math and assigned them to two different workshops. The first taught students study skills, while the second taught students about how the brain grows and develops when faced with challenges.

At the end of the semester, the students who received the growth mindset workshop improved their GPA, while the control groups' GPA actually worsened. The students in the growth mindset group "learned that the brain actually forms new connections every time you learn something new, and that over time, this makes you smarter."

When we embrace the growth mindset, we open ourselves up to the opportunity to learn and grow. It starts with our belief. Confucius once said, "He who says he can and he who says he can't are both usually right." When we think we can't do something we're right because we won't even try. However, when we think we can do something, all we have to do is figure out how.

***

This book is my answer to the question I had during coffee: What if you could have a personal trainer for your mind?

I knew I'd honed my mind to take on the World's Toughest Mudder, but I didn't understand why everything worked.

I began putting the pieces of the puzzle together and the answer that took shape shocked me.

I realized training our mind is both incredibly complex and critical to health and happiness. It involves understandings of complex science, nutrition, training, and more. It requires new ways to measure performance. It forces us to challenge long-held beliefs and re-imagine what's possible for our lives.

Training our mind doesn't mean grabbing the latest gadget or "mind training" game and hoping for the best. We aren't going to feel like Bradley Cooper in *Limitless* after trying a new brain supplement. Although, that would be pretty cool.

To understand the power of our mind, I realized I'd need to go much deeper than surface level mind training apps or mind games.

In my quest to create a guide to training our mind, I researched and interviewed Esports athletes, memory champions, chess grand masters, entrepreneurs, drone racers, psychologists, performance coaches, and more.

Mindsports athletes offer us a unique insight into how the best in the world train their minds to compete at the highest levels.

They compete and train just like other athletes, but with a special focus on the mind. When an activity is almost entirely focused on mental performance vs. physical performance, we can isolate and study the effects of tactics like exercise and nutrition on how they influence the mental side of performance.

Just like LeBron James, Tiger Woods, Serena Williams, and Conor McGregor have an army of trainers to keep their bodies performing at their peak; mindsports athletes also require training to reach peak performance.

What was fascinating and obvious from the beginning of my research was that mind training is clearly possible and extraordinarily beneficial. Yet, it remains something few of us actively do, and those who do, often miss the bigger picture.

***

I have three goals for *Hard Wired*:

1. Demystify the research and science behind mind training
2. Help you assess your current mental performance
3. Provide a practical guide for rewiring your mind

Think of me — and this book — as your own personal mind trainer.

Through my interviews, research, and analysis I established seven branches of mind development.

I took those seven branches and built a framework for training your mind I call *The Mind Skill Tree*. I looked at outcomes, like improved decision making, and worked backwards to determine the best ways to train that element.

The Mind Skill Tree includes:

1. Learning & Memory
2. Health
3. Mindset
4. Mental Toughness
5. Managing Emotions
6. Decision Making
7. Flow

This is not a quick fix, and it's not a book you'll read one time and never think of again. Much like physical training, mind training is a lifelong endeavor that is personal to you as it evolves over time.

After finishing this book you will have a mind training framework you can implement, along with a newfound appreciation for the role your brain and mind play in your life.

***

I originally set off on this journey for myself — to try to understand what I had been doing, why some things had worked and others hadn't. Along the way, I realized it's so much bigger than just me.

This book was written with students, entrepreneurs, and gamers in mind. Whether you are studying for finals, looking to make better decisions at work, or trying to manage your emotions during intense games, this book is for you. In reality, anyone interested in improving mind performance will enjoy this book.

- Would you like to be able to remember names better, important dates, test material, or even where you parked your car?
- Do you want to be able to pay better attention and comprehend new information?
- Would you like to be more social and better connect with friends, teammates, or work colleagues?
- Do you want your mind to be in good working order for the rest of your life?
- Would you like to learn how to become better at making decisions?
- Do you want to develop the mindset to achieve the things you once thought impossible?

If you answered "yes" to any of these questions, you're in luck. We will unpack how you can rewire your mind and improve your mental performance in the chapters to come.

∗∗∗

As humans, we are an ultimate adaptation machine.

We can learn new information throughout our lives thanks to brain plasticity. Our free will allows us to change the way we think about things, entirely re-framing our world. We can build-up foundational areas of our minds and work toward optimal mental performance.

Hard Wired is broken up into three parts. Part 1 introduces the concept and covers The Mind Skill Tree. In Part 2 we dive into each of the seven branches. We wrap up in Part 3 with applying the framework.

I didn't want to develop a framework full of unrealistic or unattainable ideas and tactics. That wouldn't be helpful. Instead, everything you are going to learn in this book is designed to set you up for success. You won't transform your mind overnight, but you can begin the journey right now.

Training your mind is personal. The goal is to find what works best for you. I recommend taking the lessons you learn throughout this book and adapting them to suit your needs. This will help you realize the best results possible.

2

HOW YOUR BRAIN WORKS
BRAIN SCIENCE

———

"To think is to practice brain chemistry."

– DEEPAK CHOPRA

"What do you mean we can change our minds? Doesn't everyone already know that?"

I had attempted to explain that we can change our minds, but accidentally left out the word 'physically.'

I clarified that our brains are moldable, like plastic. By changing the way think about something, we physically rewire our brain and create new connections in our mind.

"Did this help you with the Tough Mudder," asked my friend.

As I thought about his question I realized it wouldn't have been possible without rewiring my mind.

INSIDE YOUR BRAIN

Our brain is like a set of three Russian nesting dolls. The outermost doll is the largest and most intricately designed, while the innermost is the smallest and simplest, just like the layers of our brain. Over time, our brain evolved and developed into three distinct sections, all with their own purpose. They include the following:

1. Reptilian brain – Our oldest brain, this is responsible for vital functions like heartbeat and breathing.
2. Mammalian brain – Also known as the *limbic system*, the brain is responsible for emotions and memory.
3. Primate brain – Known as the *neocortex*, this is the largest and most complex part of our brain responsible for abstract thought, language, imagination, and learning.

Our brain develops over time and is made up of billions of brain cells called neurons, which process and transmit information. To keep our brain healthy and functioning at its best, we need both good blood flow and a source of energy.

Our brain uses about 20% of the blood in our body, bringing in oxygen and nutrients to keep things running smoothly. Poor blood flow can cause effects like headaches, dizziness, brain fog, and lightheadedness, which could be caused by excess weight and high blood pressure from a sedentary life-style or by constricted blood vessels from excessive caffeine consumption.

Luckily, there are some easy actions we can take to ensure our brain is getting good blood flow. Two areas to focus on include taking care of our diet and body.

Diet – Eating certain foods like fish, beets, berries, nuts, or dark chocolate can help improve blood flow. Drinking more water and reducing caffeine, alcohol, and salt consumption is also helpful.

Body – An activity that gets our blood pumping, from lifting weights to going for a short walk, is enough to improve blood flow. Getting a massage can also loosen up our body and stimulate blood flow.

Implementing simple tactics can result in a huge improvement in the healthy functioning of your brain. Just incorporating one or two of these examples into your daily routine aids with improved blood flow.

BRAIN WAVES

Our brain is an electric organ and our neurons create electrical activity when they communicate with each other. When many neurons send electric signals together, brain waves are produced. Our brain waves change according to what we are doing and how we are feeling.

Brain waves are measured in hertz (Hz) and there are four primary types: *beta, alpha, theta, and delta*. Each type of wave has its own characteristics and effects.

We don't produce just one type of brain wave at a time; our brain activity is a mix of all the frequencies at once, just in varying quantities and strengths. We can think of brain waves as musical notes – low frequency waves are like the deep sound you hear in *Jaws*, while high frequency waves are more like a flute. When higher brain waves are dominant, we can feel wired and alert, while when slower brain waves are dominant, we can feel tired and relaxed.

Understanding our different brain waves is important as it can help us shift our brain into our desired state.

While we are awake our brain is typically in a *beta wave* state *(14 – 40 Hz)*. Beta waves are associated with problem-solving and attention.

As we shift into a more relaxed state our brain gears down to alpha waves. *Alpha waves (8 – 13 Hz)* are associated with memory, learning, creativity, and focus. These waves are considered to be the gateway to the subconscious mind and are the ideal time to mold our way of thinking.

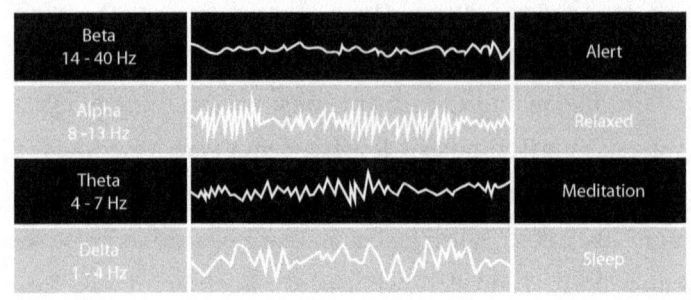

Beta 14 - 40 Hz		Alert
Alpha 8 -13 Hz		Relaxed
Theta 4 - 7 Hz		Meditation
Delta 1 - 4 Hz		Sleep

As our brain waves slow down further and enter into *theta waves (4 - 7 Hz)*. Our body begins to relax and our temperature begins to drop. If you have ever been driving on an empty highway and can't remember the last 10 miles, you likely entered a theta state. Runners also enter this state while on long stretches of trails. Good ideas often come to us during these states.

If you ever have trouble with a problem or need to think about something in a new way, putting yourself in a new mind state can help. Going for a long walk, meditating, or doing something that calms your mind puts you in a state that is more conducive to change. This is where we rewire our mind.

Our slowest brain waves are *delta waves (1 - 4 Hz)*, which occur during sleep. These waves are crucial for rejuvenation and repair. Think of this time as a mental reset for our brain.

We need all types of brain waves for optimal brain functioning and understanding these states help us be mentally productive across a variety of states, from intense focus to restful sleep.

BRAIN CHEMISTRY

If we gain control of our brain chemistry, we gain control of our life.

Chemical changes in our brain cause all of our feelings and emotions. Both the excitement we feel after passing a test and the sadness we experience after a break up are changes in brain chemistry.

Anytime our brain needs to communicate something it uses chemical messengers called *neurotransmitters* to transmit information between neurons. Our brain relies on hundreds of unique neurotransmitters, which contribute to our thoughts, speech, mood, memory, sleep, and more.

Our neurotransmitters have a profound impact on both our brain function and how we feel. If we understand how our brain chemistry influences how we feel, we can take action to regain control of our mind.

Here are a few key neurotransmitters to remember:

Dopamine – Known as the "reward or pleasure chemical," *dopamine* is involved in attention, motivation, movement, and perception.

Dopamine is about *seeking* – finding that next thing. Think about scrolling on Instagram or Facebook. We hop on the platform for a minute, but every scroll contains the possibility of something new, something to find. Our brain loves this and every time we "discover" something dopamine is released. This isn't inherently good or bad, rather something of which to be aware. If we find ourselves stuck in a negative social media discovery loop, we can interrupt it by taking an action like locking our phone and setting it down. We can also use this discovery loop to our advantage when we are reading a book, each new page has something new to discover, compelling us to continue.

Exercise also boosts dopamine, priming our attention, and improving our mood and sense of well-being. Tied to motivation and alertness, dopamine itself keeps us awake.

Serotonin – *Serotonin* is often called the "happiness neurotransmitter" and promotes relaxation and positive social interactions by decreasing aggression. It is commonly the focus of antidepressants because of its effect on improving mood and cognition.

Serotonin is also important for regulating our body's internal clock, which influences sleep, emotions, and appetite. We actually find 95% of our serotonin in our gut, which is why it is often called our *second brain*.

Two ways to increase our serotonin levels are exercise and getting more sunlight. An easy way to double dip here is to go for a walk or bike ride outside! If you are stuck inside all day or have a packed schedule, think about what you could do to get even 5 or 10 minutes of time outside or moving your body.

Norepinephrine – *Norepinephrine* affects attention, mood, arousal, and alertness. It sends signals that activate the sympathetic nervous system (fight-or-flight response), sharpening our senses, and putting us on high alert. Keeping this arousal neurotransmitter in check is important for managing anxiety.

Glutamate/GABA – Our body has both excitatory and inhibitory neurotransmitters, which either push our neurons to send signals or hold them back. Glutamate and GABA are opposing forces in our brain, excitatory vs. inhibitory, green light vs. red light. It is important both these remain balanced for normal brain function. Studies suggest that exercise may help replenish these neurotransmitters, ensuring our brain has all it needs.

BDNF – *Brain-derived neurotrophic factor* (BDNF) is not technically a neurotransmitter, rather it is a neurotrophin. Neurotrophins build up the infrastructure within our brain, cell circuitry that enables neurotransmitters to transmit signals. Without them, it would be like trying to make a call without any cell service or sending an email without an internet connection.

BDNF acts like Miracle-Gro for our brain. If you sprinkle BDNF on neurons, they will grow branches (just like the growth required for learning). BDNF protects our neurons against damage, supports their growth, and improves their function.

There are a number of ways to increase levels of BDNF, including getting better sleep, meditating, and getting more sunlight. However, if you only do one thing to boost BDNF, it would be exercise. Strength training and various forms of aerobic exercise, like running, biking, and swimming, are all great options.

REWIRE YOUR BRAIN

Our brain is adaptable, like plastic. We can mold and shape it to fit our desires thanks to the concept of *neuroplasticity.*

Think of the brain as a connected group of trails. Some trails are well traveled: these are our habits and established ways of doing things. Every time we practice a task, feel an emotion, or think a certain way, we clear the trail and make it easy for our brain to use this pathway.

When we start thinking about things in a new way or begin a new task, we head down another path. This trail is the road less traveled, full of sticks, plants, and trees. We need to clear the trail and carve out a new path. The more we use this path the easier it becomes to travel and our new way of thinking becomes second nature. When we stop using the old trail, it becomes overgrown and the pathways weaken.

Strengthening New Connections

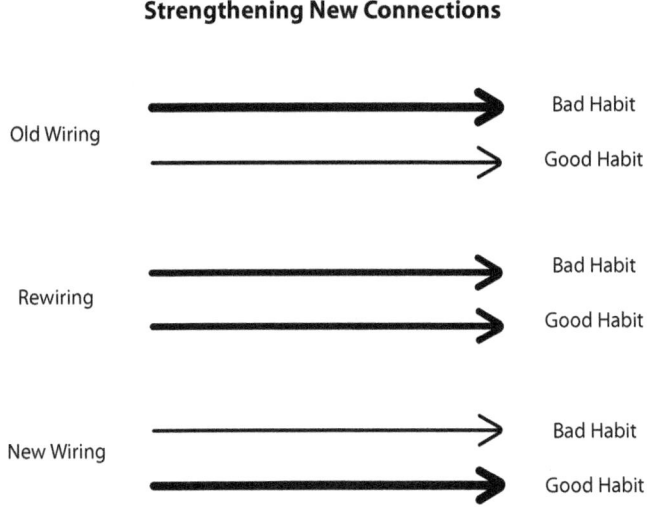

This process of, forming new connections and weakening old ones, is how we rewire our brains. Anytime we build a new habit or change how we think about something we rewire our brains and experience neuroplasticity in action.

There is a saying that goes, neurons that fire together, wire together. The key to learning and forming new connections in our brain occurs through a mechanism known as *long-term potentiation* (LTP). LTP strengthens the connections of our neurons, which makes it easier to transmit information.

Think about our name, phone number, or home address. We have had to recall this information so many times that our brains become efficient at recalling this information.

Through repeated activity our neurons form stronger connections and become capable of sending signals more quickly. This is thanks to a process called *myelination*.

Myelin is a fatty layer of insulation that surrounds all of our neurons. "With the repetition, you're creating thicker myelin around nerve fibers, which improves the quality and the speed of the signals, and in turn, the circuit's efficiency," explained John Ratey, MD, an Associate Clinical Professor of Psychiatry at Harvard.

One area we see this play out is Esports.

Professional gamers often display amazing feats of speed. Players in Fortnite can build huge structures in the blink of an eye and League of Legends pros can pull off a string of amazing skill combos without making a mistake. It seems like their brains are wired differently.

While pro gamers' brains likely are wired differently, they didn't start out this way. As players gain experience, their brains become more efficient at processing information and sending signals to react. "Information is transferred sub-consciously when you play. Getting into familiar situations triggers your muscle memory and decision making ability," explained EAthlete Labs.

Think about trying something new for the first time. It could be playing an instrument, trying a sport, or starting a new video game. When you first get started it takes a long time to process basic information and reactions are slow. However, as you practice and become better at processing information, your reaction times improve as well.

This is the same process pro gamers go through and it comes back to the process of myelination.

A myelinated neuron sends signals 100 times faster than uninsulated neurons. Myelination also reduces the time it takes neurons to send additional signals by a factor of 30. This combination boosts information processing and reaction speed by a factor of 3000.

Through repetition and hundreds of hours of practice, pro gamers rewire their brains to be able to process information at rapid speeds. They establish strong mental connections that translate into automatic decision making, just as we don't have to think when asked what our name is.

We can rewire our brains to change the way we think and make it automatic just like pro gamers. It simply requires focusing our attention toward a desired change and strengthening that connection over time through repetition.

∗∗∗

The process of rewiring your brain is the foundation for everything that follows in this book. Each chapter builds on this concept and adds new skills and ideas to hard wire into your mind. The importance of neuroplasticity cannot be understated. You have the power to rewire your mind.

KEY TAKEAWAYS

- We can change our mental state by changing our brainwaves and brain chemistry. Exercise, sleep, sunlight, and meditation are all powerful tools we can use to regain control of our thoughts and how we feel.
- Thanks to neuroplasticity, our brains can physically change, reorganizing themselves to form new connections.
- We can rewire our brain by changing the way we think and the way we do things. Each time we use a pathway our brain becomes stronger and the action or thought becomes hard wired within us.

3

A NEW MIND
THE MIND SKILL TREE

———

"The whole is greater than the sum of its parts."

– ARISTOTLE

"Big rocks and pebbles hold the secret to building a new mind."

My friend stared blankly back at me.

I continued, "Our life is like an empty jar. We can fill it up with both big rocks and pebbles. If we start with the pebbles, all of the big rocks will never all fit. However, if we put the big rocks in first, everything else can fall into place."

Big rocks are the things that are most important in our lives.

My friend nodded.

I explained that the same idea applies to rewiring our mind. In the beginning, we should focus on big rocks, foundational mental skills, as they will have the biggest impact. Once we take care of the big rocks, there is room to grow and expand our mind as we fill in the jar with pebbles.

HORMESIS

We often use stress to describe how we feel, however it takes on new meaning when we look at it from a biological perspective. "Stress is a threat to the body's equilibrium. It's a challenge to react, a call to adapt," explained John Ratey.

Stress can either kill us or make us stronger. Stress itself could be the solution to our stress.

There is one type of stress we do not want: *chronic stress.*

From an evolutionary perspective, stress is a good thing. If we encountered a hungry lion in the wild and needed to escape, our body would release "stress hormones" like cortisol, adrenaline, and norepinephrine. These hormones help pass along a message to our body to stop whatever it is doing and put all its resources into thinking and moving fast. In the lion example, our brain and muscles fire up, ready to go.

While this response can be life saving, it can also cause problems in our modern day society as our body has a hard time differentiating between physical threats and mental ones.

Chronic stress is our emotional response to prolonged periods of pressure on our body and mind. This kind of stress comes from bad relationships, financial struggles, overly demanding jobs, and excessive exercise.

Physical stress often has a clear end, whereas psychological stress has no definite end, so our stress hormones stay elevated in our body for prolonged periods.

Chronic stress keeps our cortisol levels elevated, taking energy from our muscles and moving it to our belly as a protective mechanism, which turns into fat. A big gut and slender arms and legs may be a sign someone is experiencing chronic stress. Additional side effects include excess inflammation, tense muscles, pain, depression, and a weakened immune system. With 8 out of 10 Americans afflicted by stress throughout the day, it is no wonder stress is called a silent killer.

However, not all stress is bad. One type of stress serves as the foundation for growth: *acute stress*.

Acute stress is the good kind of stress.

Controlled bouts of stress, done periodically, encourage growth, bolster our resilience, and improve our body's ability to respond to stress – making us stronger.

Lifting weights to get stronger, fasting to strengthen our body, studying an extra hour to learn more, or taking on a challenging level in a video game are all forms of positive acute stress.

As the Old Testament says in Proverbs 27:17, "As iron sharpens iron, so one person sharpens another." This concept is called *hormesis*.

Hormesis is the phenomenon and mechanism where low-dose stressors produce a beneficial effect and high-dose stressors produce a harmful or toxic effect. Small doses of temporary stress in the form of working out, fasting, studying, or working though a challenging problem cause our body to adapt and grow stronger, so we can handle future challenges.

Fitness author and ancestral health authority Mark Sisson writes, "Best of all, you don't just compensate for the stressor.

You *super compensate*. You get stronger/faster/healthier/more resistant to disease than you were before. Think of hormesis as your body 'hedging its bet' and going a little above and beyond just to be safe."

While we need stress to grow, we don't grow during periods of stress, rather we grow while we rest. There is a simple formula to all growth:

$$Stress + Rest = Growth$$

All skill development starts with struggle. We can use this knowledge to master any skill we want. This is exactly what Josh Waitzkin did- – twice.

It started with his first love at 6 years old: chess.

Waitzkin was walking with his mother through Washington Square Park in New York City and intended to play on the monkey bars, but was instead drawn to games of chess being played by street hustlers in the park.

Waitzkin threw himself into the game and quickly began making a name for himself. Word spread of his talents and there was no shortage of chess masters ready to mentor him.

As his formal training picked up, Waitzkin began his domination of the US junior chess scene and by age nine was already winning national chess championships. At 16, he became an International Master and was crowned the US Junior co-champion- – an impressive feat for anyone, especially in a bracket that included contenders up to 21 years old. That following year Waitzkin became the outright champion.

Despite his passion for the game, Waitzkin's success in chess did not come without struggle.

"Growth comes at the point of resistance. We learn by pushing ourselves and finding what really lies at the outer reaches of our abilities," explained Waitzkin. This might sound like an intense workout at the gym, but this is the process he used to master the game of chess.

While practicing chess Waitzkin would push his mind to the limit, often to the edge of utter exhaustion. Without stressing his mind, Waitzkin would never have been able to improve his ability to the point he did. Without stress, there is no growth.

In his early 20s, despite his success and fame, Waitzkin's interests began to shift and he transitioned away from chess. He was drawn to Eastern philosophy and meditation, which led him to the Chinese martial art of Tai Chi.

Just as in chess, Waitzkin began rising in the martial arts world and started making a name for himself. Martial arts masters became interested in coaching and mentoring him. It didn't take long for Waitzkin to amass numerous national championships. Before he was 30, Waitzkin was crowned world champion in both fixed step push hands and moving step push hands, the main competitive forms of Tai Chi.

How was Waitzkin able to rise to the top in two completely distinct fields? One simple formula: stress + rest = growth.

"If you are interested in really improving as a performer, I would suggest incorporating the rhythm of stress and recovery into all aspects of your life," explained Waitzkin.

Waitzkin was able to take the same philosophy he used to train his mind and apply it to training his body for Tai Chi. Struggle is inevitable, but deep learning comes from those mistakes. The reason Waitzkin was able to constantly improve was because he practiced *productive failure.*

Science has found that our greatest learning occurs when we are challenged and fail. Struggling and failing provides an opportunity for us to analyze a problem from multiple perspectives and learn *why* we failed. Once we internalize this knowledge, we can take it and use it the next time we encounter a challenge so we can overcome it.

***

While we need to stress ourselves in order to grow, we can't forget about the other side of the equation: rest.

We need balance. Too much stress without enough rest, limits our growth.

Josh Hafkin, former Olympic trials swimmer and founder of the Game Gym (an Esports gym for young people) understands how this applies to both our mind and body.

"I can only physically run for so long. Despite my mind wanting to go further, my body will no longer be able to take me there," explained Hafkin, "In Esports it's the opposite. Your mind tires, but because we are not taught how to recognize those symptoms, people play video games too long."

We need to take time to recover so that stress does not overwhelm us. Our rest and recovery can take many forms including: walking, sleeping, meditating, getting out in nature, unplugging from technology, or spending time with friends and family. Anything that helps us to recover after stress counts as rest.

Researchers at Bangor University in the UK found that athletes who reviewed game performance in a social, relaxed atmosphere had higher ratios of testosterone to cortisol (an indicator of systemic recovery) than athletes who did not. This laid back atmosphere was a critical part of recovery for the athletes.

When we take time to relax, we change our mental state, just like shifting our brainwaves from beta to alpha. Our body and mind need time to rest after working hard.

However, we can take rest too far in the other direction as well. If all we do is rest we can't expect to grow. We need to find balance.

We can learn the secret to maximizing growth and achieving optimal performance, in any endeavor, from the story of Goldilocks. The secret is finding *The Goldilocks Zone*.

Goldilocks found porridge that wasn't too hot and wasn't too cold; it was *just right*. We need just the right amount of stress and rest to grow.

With too little stress, we fail to grow and under-perform because we are bored and not challenged enough. This would be like an NBA team scrimmaging against a high school JV team.

However, we can take things too far and push ourselves if we aren't ready for the challenge yet. Imagine trying to squat 500 lb without any experience in weight lifting. The weight would crush us.

We need just the right amount of stress to grow and perform at our best.

The Performance Arousal Curve serves as a good visual. This curve is based on the Yerkes-Dodson law that states- – *"increased levels of arousal will improve performance, but only up until the optimum arousal level is reached. At that point, performance begins to suffer as arousal levels increase."*

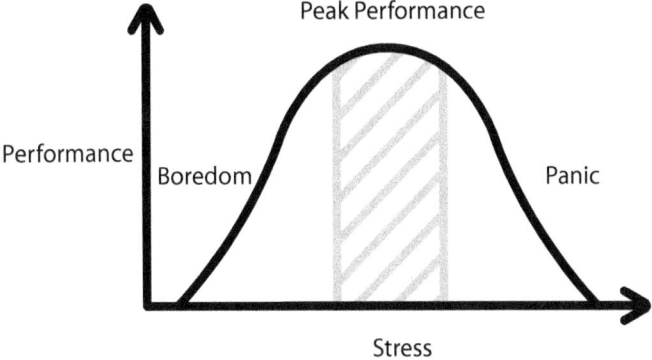

Hafkin explained, "Most gamers spend a majority of their practice time on the right half of the bell curve. It is dangerous. You are not practicing in your best head space, you create bad habits, and become frustrated."

Anytime we are trying to learn something new and grow, we must pause and think where we are on this curve. If we feel bored, we need to turn up the challenge. If we feel overwhelmed, we need to dial things back. We need to find what is just right for us.

THE WHOLE IS GREATER

The ancient Greek philosopher Aristotle might have been on to something when he said, "The whole is greater than the sum of its parts."

Think about a computer. There is a key board, screen, mouse, speakers, chips, wires, software, and a host of additional components that help make up the final product of a computer. Each piece on their own has value, but when we put them all together, we create something even more valuable.

The same concept applies to books. Books are made up of individual chapters, but it doesn't become valuable until they are all pieced together.

Training our mind is just like putting a book together. Learning how to make better decisions and control our emotions are both beneficial on their own, but we'll see the best results when we bring everything together.

To see the best results we should focus on improving all the aspects of performance together.

However, where do we start? We can't focus on everything at once so we need a way to prioritize.

The easiest method for prioritization is to use the 80/20 rule, AKA Pareto's Principle. The rule states that 80% of our results come from 20% of our effort, and vice versa. The idea is to look for the big rocks that will yield the greatest results and start there.

For example, a professional biking team would first focus on finding top tier bikes, developing a training program, and having a good nutrition plan. Addressing these big rocks makes a huge difference and gets us 80% of the way there, but sometimes the 80% is not enough to win. We shouldn't ignore the importance of all the little things or the value in making tiny improvements either. These small changes can make a big difference.

In 2002, the British cycling team was a disaster. It had been a disaster since 1908, having won only one Olympic gold medal in that time. The Brits had the same luck with the Tour de France, with zero wins in 110 years. Enter Sir Dave Brailsford. Brailsford was hired as the performance director for British Cycling to turn the team around.

Brailsford, a former professional cyclist, brought a radical new concept to the team: *the aggregation of marginal gains.*

"The whole principle came from the idea that if you broke down everything you could think of that goes into riding a bike and then improve it by 1%, you will get a significant increase when you put them all together," explained Brailsford.

The team began searching for 1% improvement in everything they did; nothing was off limits. The team hired a surgeon to teach the athletes how to best wash their hands in order to avoid getting sick. They tested how aerodynamic their suits were to maximize their efficiency when outside. During competition, the support team would even go to the hotel the racers were staying at and replace the bedding and pillows with the bedding each athlete was used to so they would sleep with the same posture each night.

The tiny improvements paid off.

In 2008, at the Beijing Olympics, the British track and cycling team took home 8 gold medals. They followed up their stand-up Olympic performance in 2012 with 8 more gold medals, including 7 world records at the London Olympics.

In 2012 Bradley Wiggins went on to become the first ever British winner of the Tour de France. Chris Froome, won the Tour de France in 2013, 2015, 2016, and 2017. Not too shabby for a bunch of 1% improvements.

A 1% improvement may not seem like much, but over time, the actions have a compounding effect. It is like cutting out 100 calories of food each day when trying to lose weight. At first, we won't notice much, but after a few months we will see changes.

James Clear, habit expert and author of *Atomic Habits*, highlights the idea of "The Power of Tiny Gains." The message behind this idea is simple; get a little better every day.

The Power of Tiny Gains

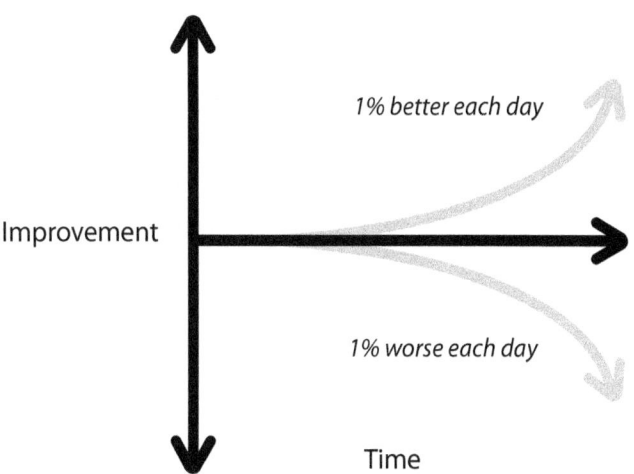

When we combine the idea that the whole is greater than the sum of its parts, the 80/20 rule, and the concept of 1% improvements, we can experience exponential growth.

Now it is time to bring it all together and discover what it looks like to train our mind with The Mind Skill Tree.

THE MIND SKILL TREE

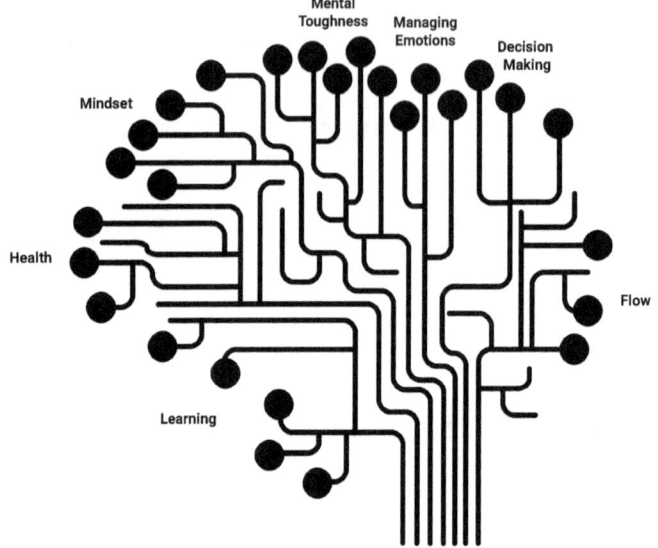

Skill trees are commonly found in role playing video games (RPG) like *Skyrim*, *The Witcher*, and *Assassin's Creed*. A skill tree has a set of skills and abilities that branch out into different paths once we complete and unlock prerequisite skills. Each foundational element can be leveled up individually or in conjunction with other skills. The beauty of a skill tree is we can focus on whatever skill is most interesting to us.

I wanted a tangible framework to organize the principles for training our minds. Thus, The Mind Skill Tree was created. It is built upon foundational principles and abilities of a strong mind.

There are seven branches of The Mind Skill Tree, each focused on a unique element of our mind. Each chapter in part 2 will cover these seven branches as you learn about how to train each element and rewire your mind.

Each branch of the skill tree starts out with basic skills. As you master basic skills, you can progress onto more challenging skills.

Let's use managing emotions as an example. There are stages of skill development through which we progress. On this branch of the tree, we first learn about the emotional spectrum and how this looks. As we progress, we learn how to become aware of our emotions and identify where we are on the spectrum at any given moment. Lastly, we can work on controlling our emotions so we can move along the spectrum, back towards balance.

As we work on developing and training our mind, the skills we learn become ingrained within us. They become hard wired.

Let's use mental toughness to illustrate this point. Say you wanted to get up at 4 a.m. five days a week to go to the gym, but struggle to get out of bed before 6:30. There are a few steps you can take to rewire your brain and solidify the connection for this behavior. Start small and set your alarm for

6:15 and practice waking up a little earlier. You might need to go to sleep a little earlier to help get up in morning, but each time you do get up at 6:15, you build up your mental toughness muscle.

Once 6:15 becomes comfortable, it is time to set your alarm for 6:00. After a few more weeks and months of getting up a little earlier and earlier, you will be getting up at 4 a.m. no problem. Each step of the way, that new behavior becomes hard wired in your mind so you can move on to the next level and take on new challenges. The possibilities of how to use this skill tree are endless.

Each branch of the skill tree is part of an interconnected system that we can use to strengthen our entire mind. Each skill is complementary. Decision making and managing emotions are two skills that have significant overlap. We can't train one, without benefiting the other.

Together, we will advance along The Mind Skill Tree to rewire our minds.

KEY TAKEAWAYS

- Stress + rest (hormesis) is the key to growth and peak performance. This is true in any endeavor.

- Combining the idea that the whole is greater than the sum of its parts, the 80/20 rule, and the concept of 1% improvements is the key to exponential growth.
- There are 7 branches of The Mind Skill Tree. The skills outlined in each branch provide a roadmap for rewiring our mind.

4

THE ULTIMATE SUPERPOWER

LEARNING

———

"Study the science of art. Study the art of science. Develop your senses — especially learn how to see. Realize that everything connects to everything else."

— LEONARDO DA VINCI

"Your ability to learn is your greatest superpower."

"Why's that?" asked my friend.

"Learning is a meta skill," I explained, "A meta skill is a master skill that serves as a catalyst for acquiring new skills. Learning how to learn enables us to more effectively acquire new skills because we understand the foundational process behind effective learning."

We all have the capacity to learn, but the ability to learn is a skill.

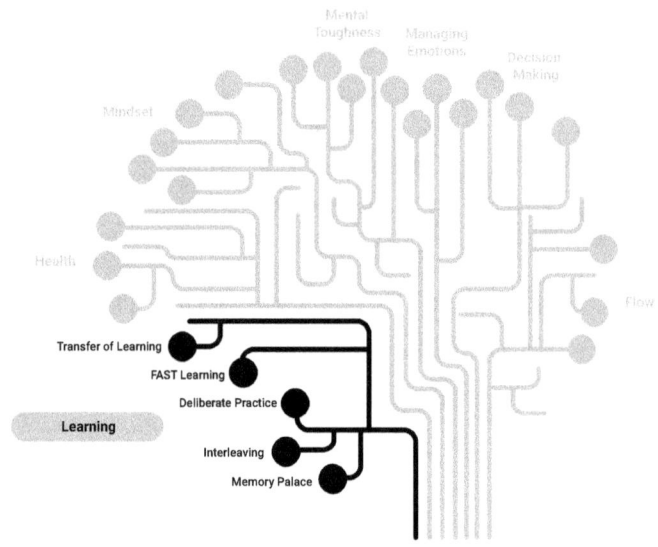

LEARNING

Being a jack of all trades isn't always celebrated. We often here the saying, "A jack of all trades is a master of none." We are told that we should only ever pursue one interest to be successful.

However, that is not the whole saying. It really goes like this, "A jack of all trades is a master of none, but oftentimes better than a master of one."

Not only is it possible to be a jack of all trades and become successful, but it may hold the secret to learning and creativity.

Just look at Elon Musk.

Musk built three multi-billion dollar companies, in three different fields, all before turning 50. How did he build companies like Space X (aerospace), SolarCity (energy), and Tesla (transportation)? Musk studied diverse fields and built expertise in a broad array of topics. By doing this, he embraced the idea of "a jack of all trades" and became an *Expert Generalist.*

Orit Gadiesh, chairman of Bain & Company describes an expert generalist as, "Someone who has the ability and curiosity to master and collect expertise in many different disciplines, industries, skills, capabilities, countries, and topics., etc. He or she can then, without necessarily even realizing it, but often by design:

1. Draw on that palette of diverse knowledge to recognize patterns and connect the dots across multiple areas.
2. Drill deep to focus and perfect the thinking."

Expert generalists can quickly adapt to change, make connections which would otherwise be ignored, and look at problems with a broader worldview. To develop these skills expert generalists become expert learners.

Musk started his learning journey as a teenager. His brother, Kimbal Musk, said he would read two books a day on topics from programming, business, energy, philosophy, and more.

Transfer is the reason this worked so well for Musk.

Transfer is the ability to extend what you learned in one context to new contexts. It comes in multiple forms such as *near transfer* (similar contexts) and *far transfer* (seemingly unrelated contexts). For this to work, we need a solid understanding of one topic before applying it somewhere else.

This is crucial, as all new learning requires transfer from previous experiences, aka our memory.

"You can't learn without memorizing, and if done right, you can't memorize without learning," explained Joshua Foer, author of *Moonwalking with Einstein*. Our ability to recall information is foundational to learning. We can't use transfer effectively if we can't draw on information we don't remember. This requires committing information to memory.

Improving our memory helps us to move between ideas and build new connections just like Musk.

Musk is able to effectively utilize transfer in his life because of his focus on understanding the core elements vs. simply memorizing information. He explained, "It is important to view knowledge as sort of a semantic tree — make sure you understand the fundamental principles, i.e. the trunk and big branches, before you get into the leaves/details or there is nothing for them to hang onto."

The same thinking applies to our Mind Skill Tree. Before we reach for the skills on the outer branches, it is imperative that we start with the basics. Although it might be tempting to dive into interesting details, we need a solid foundational understanding of core principles first.

To understand the fundamental principles, first explore a variety of approaches, deconstruct them, and analyze them. Then we can compare and contrast them to our previous knowledge and apply them to new areas.

The magic behind this is as you continually learn new skills, you develop the skill of learning itself. When you are constantly challenged to understand new topics, you develop effective ways to grasp new concepts.

Musk took the principles he learned from engineering and applied them to technology to build companies, which push the bounds of industry, like SpaceX and Tesla. The core idea behind this element of learning transfer is to build connections and draw parallels between two things.

As you learn about new topics, ask yourself, "What does it remind me of, and why?" Even if nothing instantly comes to mind, stretch yourself and practice building those connections.

FAST LEARNING

World renowned learning and memory expert, Jim Kwik developed the FAST learning model to learn any subject or skill in half the time.

F (Forget) – The first step is to forget what you already know. Go into learning with a beginner›s mindset: there is always something new to learn because you don't know what you don't know. When you embrace being a beginner again, it opens you up to new learning.

A (Active) – We experience information overload on a daily basis and are exposed to more than 5,000 ads on any given day. We consume information all day long at school, work, and home. However just consuming information is not the best way to learn.

The problem is "your brain does not learn through consumption, it learns through creation," explained Kwik. Don't sit back as a passive spectator and expect to learn. We need to take an active approach to learning: participate, pay attention, and take notes.

S (State) – "Information + Emotion = Long-Term Memory," explained Kwik.

Think back to the smell of fresh cookies at grandma's house, your first kiss, or getting your college acceptance letter. Those memories stuck with you because they were paired with strong emotions. Compare that to how you felt in school. Sitting through 6th period history, bored out of your mind, is not ideal for learning.

You can control your learning state in two simple ways:

1. Create an environment conducive for learning
2. Find something you are excited to learn about!

T (Teach) – Seneca, the Roman philosopher, said, "While we teach, we learn." You will retain information better when you go in with the intent to teach what you learned. When you teach, you get to learn the information twice which helps to imprint it in your memory.

PLAY LIKE YOU PRACTICE

Malcolm Gladwell popularized Anders Ericcson's concept of the 10,000-hour rule in his book *Outliers*. It takes on average 10,000 hours of practice to become an expert.

There is a caveat. It takes on average 10,000 hours of *deliberate practice* to become an expert. Deliberate practice is an intentional and systematic approach with the goal of improving performance.

Growing up, my basketball coaches always said, "You play like you practice." When we were sloppy and lazy in practice it showed in our games.

You can put in 10,000 hours of "practice," but you won't get better unless you practice with purpose. When you just go through the motions that is as good as you will ever be.

In order to understand expertise better, let's look at chess grandmasters.

Grandmasters are not any smarter than the average person is. So what separates these experts from average players?

Grandmasters see the world differently. They automatically react to important information, rather than spending a long time thinking. This is the reason memory is the best indicator of chess expertise.

Ericcson explains expertise is, "vast amounts of knowledge, pattern-based retrieval, and planning mechanisms acquired over many years of experience in the associated domain. Experts do not just end up with a great memory because of the time they spend working; their great memories are a fundamental component of their expertise."

Grandmasters can memorize boards immediately and can visualize previous games they have watched or played. During matches, researchers found grandmasters' frontal and parietal cortices were especially active, the part of the brain responsible for long-term memory. This skill becomes so basic for experts that they can play multiple games at once, while blindfolded!

***

Nevertheless, here is the reality. Grandmasters didn't wake up one day with an amazing memory. They had to work at it and overcome the OK plateau.

When we are learning something new or practicing a new skill, we improve until we reach the OK plateau (a phrase popularized by Joshua Foer). When we hit the OK plateau, we say "good enough" and stop consciously trying to improve. Research backs this up, finding that once a task becomes automatic, the area of our brain responsible for conscious thought becomes less active.

Experts have mastered the art of purposeful practice, and they know how to stay out of the automatic stage of thinking.

Ericcson found experts have 3 primary strategies to help stay out of this stage:

1. Focusing on technique
2. Staying goal-oriented
3. Receiving immediate feedback

Stay focused on the task at hand and consciously think about what you are doing when you practice. If you catch yourself getting distracted, bring yourself back to the present and refocus. If you can't, take a break and come back later when you feel refreshed. (More on how to be present in chapter 6)

If you are still stuck on autopilot, increase the difficulty. Push yourself out of your comfort zone. This will require your full attention to perform at your best.

You will make mistakes and struggle when you push yourself, but adversity teaches you what areas you need to work on in order improve. You can cut down the hours it takes to learn something new when you practice deliberately.

MAKE IT STICK

What if I told you it was possible to improve your test scores dramatically without any additional studying. It just comes down to how you organize your learning.

When we begin to study for a test or learn a new skill, we typically follow a blocked pattern of practice. Blocked practice consists of tackling one topic at a time, covering it thoroughly, and then moving on to the next topic. First, we tackle skill 1, then skill 2, and finally skill 3 – which would look like this 111222333.

The strategy of blocking seems intuitive, logical, and easy to schedule. It has been the method of teaching in schools for more than a century. However, it is not the only way to learn.

Interleaving is the process of switching up your focus every now and then to prevent your brain from going on autopilot. When you interleave, you mix up/spiral the topics you are studying in order to improve learning and "forget less."

Instead of covering topics 1, 2, and 3 one at a time, interleaving consists of practicing each area together like 123123123. For instance, a basketball player might alternate between free throws, dribbling, and 3-pointers, while a student studying exercise science might switch between anatomy, nutrition, and psychology during a study session.

***

We have traditionally followed a massed learning approach in school. We spend 2 weeks learning everything we need to know about a unit, take a test to show we know it, check it off the to-do list, and then move on. When we try to come back to what we learned, there are crickets chirping in our heads.

Think about a big exam you had in high school or college. After some procrastination, you are left with one week to prepare. What do you do?

You buckle down and cram everything you possibly need to know into that noggin of yours. On test day, you feel well prepared and pass: Woohoo! You learned the material... or did you?

Imagine 2 weeks down the road you get a surprise quiz on everything that you covered for that test. Uh oh! The crickets are back. You may have stored the information temporarily, but you did not learn it.

This is why interleaving and spaced learning is so important. It is designed to make learning stick.

When we compare massed vs. spaced learning, we find spaced practice is more effective. Students can better recall information they learned from spaced learning.

During mass practice, we store information in our short-term memory primarily because it is sufficient for our current needs. However, when we interleave topics our brain has to continually bring in the information we need into our memory. Instead of mindlessly rereading information, interleaving helps reinforce connections in our brain.

It is interesting that we have known about this revolutionary way of teaching and studying since 1885, yet it is not common practice.

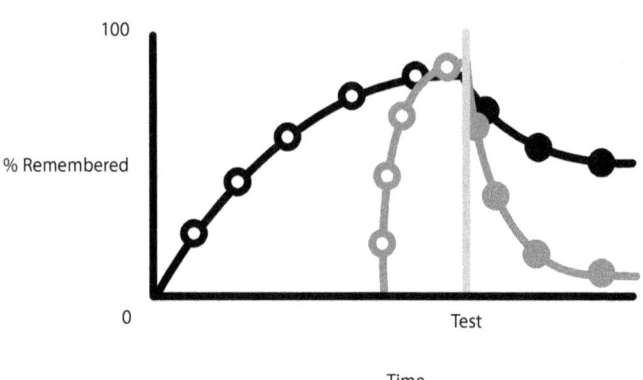

Spaced Learning

In 2014 cognitive psychologist, Doug Roher studied the effects of blocked practice vs. interleaved practice in 7th grade math classes. The students were split into the two practice styles for three months. Roher waited a few weeks after the 3 months of practice were complete and gave the students a surprise test.

The average score for the blocked practice group was 38%, while the interleaved group had an average score of 72%! With real world classroom results like this, we should be taking a close look at how to incorporate interleaving into our learning.

There is a simple secret behind interleaving's effectiveness, but once I tell you it might not seem like a good idea anymore. The reason it works is that it takes effort.

When we alternate topics during practice, we spend more time consciously learning and our brain has to work harder to differentiate between concepts and search for solutions. Interleaving helps us hone in on the core concepts and principles (like transfer), enabling us to better solve problems.

Spaced learning and interleaving takes more planning and effort, but it comes with better results.

We can apply these strategies anytime we want to learn something and make sure it sticks. A perfect opportunity to apply these strategies would be while preparing for a college final or another certification test.

There are a two pieces of information we need to know- – when our test is and what material we need to know. From there we can work backwards to space out the most important topics. We should set aside time each week to study and restudy each section leading up to the exam.

To make this even more effective we can add interleaving. Instead of studying the same topics in the same order each week, we can mix them up. This requires us to work harder, but it helps us see information in a new light and make connections we otherwise would have missed.

If we follow this strategy leading up to test day, we will have a better chance of remembering everything we need to pass.

ENTER THE MEMORY PALACE

There once was a Greek poet named Simonides. As a poet, Simonides needed an excellent memory as he had to recite poems from memory in front of crowds. One day he was hired by a wealthy nobleman to recite poetry at a banquet he was hosting. If you wanted to throw a rocking party in ancient Greece, you needed a poet. Simonides was the equivalent of your 21st century DJ.

During the party Simonides recited a poem from memory to the guests in the banquet hall. After he finished, two young men requested his presence outside. As soon as Simonides exited the hall, the roof collapsed, killing everyone inside and mangling them beyond recognition. Families and loved ones were devastated with no way to recognize the bodies.

However, Simonides could help. He was able to use his memory to recreate the scene of the hall, visualize the order of the guests, and see exactly where they were sitting. One by one, he took each family by the hand to a different spot in the rubble to find their loved one. He continued with this until every buried guest was accounted for.

Simonides discovered that order gives distinctiveness to memory. He realized that anyone who wanted to improve their memory should visualize a familiar place in their mind and put things they wish to remember in that place, keeping them in an arranged order. This order of places would help preserve the order of other things in memory.

This understanding helped Simonides become the first person to teach the art of memory and use the memory palace (AKA method of loci).

***

Simonides discovered an important fact about our memory. While many aspects of our memory may be spotty, we seem to be naturally gifted with spatial memory.

London taxi drivers are required to develop *The Knowledge* before they can become licensed drivers. They must learn 320 routes and around 20,000 different monuments/locations in London to pass the licensing exam, which can include questions on any one of the more than 25,000 streets. Training can take from 2-4 years before a trainee can take the test to become licensed.

In 2000, Eleanor Maguire of University College London studied the brains of taxi drivers to see if there was any effect from driving through the London maze. Using MRI technology she found London taxi drivers had a larger posterior hippocampus compared to the control subjects by about seven percent. The growth correlated with the amount of time spent driving as the taxi drivers continually developed their spatial memory for their jobs. Basically, they developed their own built-in Google Maps to get around London.

Luckily, we don't need to spend years of taxi driving to take advantage of our spatial memory. We can use the technique of Simonides, modern day memory champions, and Sherlock Holmes to master our memory.

Meet Alex Mullen. He is the Lebron James of memory sports.

As a full-time medical student, Mullen needed to be able to recall a lot of information. After watching a TED Talk by Joshua Foer, Mullen began experimenting with memory techniques like the memory palace to see how they could help him in school.

Shortly after he began dabbling in memory, he decided to enter the World Memory Championship. Something about memory training clicked and Mullen burst onto the scene, climbing the ranks to become the No. 1 ranked memory competitor in the world and winning the World Memory Championship 3 times (2015, 2016, & 2017).

Mullen uses the same technique as Simonides and Benedict Cumberbatch in *Sherlock*, the memory palace, when he needs to recall information.

The memory palace is a memory technique used like a map to find your way to any information you need to remember. Our brain is great at remembering visuals, but terrible with words and numbers. The memory palace helps us take information our brain isn't good at remembering and transform it into more compatible memories. It essentially helps us add context to otherwise meaningless information.

Let's try this out. We are going to create a shopping list.

Here is our shopping list:

- An apple
- A loaf of bread
- A tricycle
- A red flannel shirt
- The new Call of Duty game

This is not an average weekly shopping list, but we are out of paper and need to make sure to remember everything on the list. This is where our memory palace comes in.

First, we need to choose where our memory palace will be. This should be a familiar space. It can be any place you want like your house, your school, or a fictional place. We are going to place mental images that carry some meaning at specific loci (locations) in our memory palace.

Let's use a house as our memory palace. Within our house, we need 5 loci for each item on our shopping list. Each loci should be distinct from other loci. I find it most helpful to follow a logical order and flow, like I am walking through the memory palace.

Remembering dull, boring information is challenging for our brain so it helps to make the images or things we want to remember as weird and memorable as possible. If you saw a purple cow while driving you'd probably remember it. The crazier the things we see the more likely we are to remember them, which also makes memory a test of creativity.

Let's begin placing items at loci in our memory palace.

As you walk up to your house you look at your door and right next to it is a giant red *apple (Item #1)*. It is huge, at least 20 feet tall and there is a giant pink worm wriggling its way out of it. You open the door and sitting on your couch is a large load of *bread (Item #2)*. It has googly eyes and is jumping up and down, excited for you to be home. You look up and careening out of the living room comes a 500 lb sumo wrestler, honking a little horn, riding a tiny *tricycle (Item #3)*. As you walk into the kitchen there is a large lumberjack and a blue ox preparing dinner. He is wearing a *red flannel shirt (Item #4)* and using his ax to slice carrots on your cutting board. But your attention is quickly drawn back to the living room as you hear crackling gunfire and explosions. In your living room you have a full on war zone with each side fighting over the shining prize in the middle, *Call of Duty (Item #5)*.

The example might seem silly, but it makes it a lot easier to remember your list.

Without looking back up at the list or story, try to recall all of the items.

Did it work? If not, that's okay, it takes a little practice.

You can use your own memory palace to study for a test, prepare for a speech, remember names, or plan your grocery list. You might be thinking that your brain doesn't work like this, which is a valid concern, but remember, having a good memory doesn't just happen; it takes effort.

The harder you work, the easier it gets. Learning is our ultimate superpower, so take advantage of this fantastic gift.

KEY TAKEAWAYS

- As you learn about new topics, ask yourself, "What does it remind me of, and why?" Even if nothing instantly comes to mind, stretch yourself and practice building those connections.

- We learn best through creation. Embrace the beginner's mindset and take an active approach to learning. When you do this, your mind is open to learning new things and what you do learn will stick. Take notes, participate in discussion, and eliminate distractions like your phone when it is time to learn.

- The OK plateau is a natural part of learning. To overcome this plateau you must engage in deliberate practice. Focus on your technique, attempt challenges beyond your skill level, and ask for feedback.

- When we interleave our learning, it sticks better. Instead of reading through flashcards in the same order each time, mix them up. Cycle through the subjects you are studying instead of learning only one thing at time.

- Building a memory palace is about taking information that is hard to remember and turning it into something our brain is good at remembering. Choose a location for your memory palace and try remembering a list of 5-10 things to start.

5

HEALTHY BODY, HEALTHY MIND

BRAIN HEALTH

———

"A healthy body means a healthy mind. You get your heart rate up, and you get the blood flowing through your body to your brain. Look at Albert Einstein. He rode a bicycle. He was also an early student of Jazzercise. You never saw Einstein lift his shirt, but he had a six-pack under there."

— STEVE CARELL

"Do you think Einstein had a six pack?" I asked.

My friend almost choked while taking a sip of coffee.

"What?" I laughed. "Wouldn't it make sense that one of the greatest minds to ever live would also take care of his body?"

Regardless of how much Einstein actually exercised, we know there is a connection between our body and mind. Taking care of our body directly impacts the health of our brain.

What we eat, how well we sleep, and how much we move all play a role in rewiring our mind.

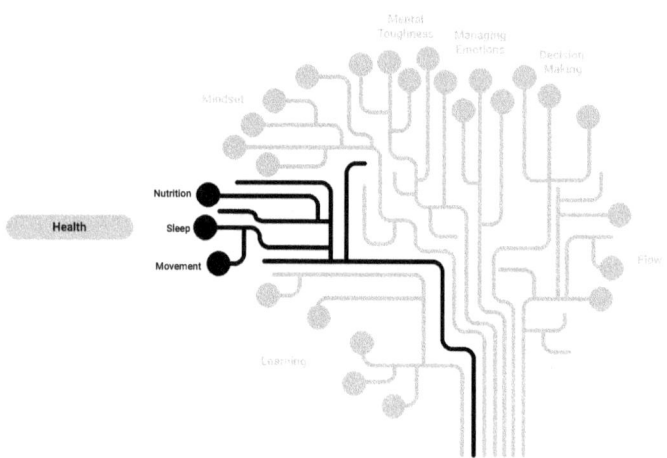

EAT

In 2011, Cavin Balaster fell 20 feet from scaffolding set up next to a water tower, hitting his head on a steel beam and crashing onto a concrete roof below. Balaster was rushed to the ER and put on life support. Doctors diagnosed him with a severe traumatic brain injury (TBI). Balaster remained in a coma with unlikely odds of coming out of it. 90% of patients with his injury ever regain consciousness.

But he did.

Balaster woke with memory loss, brain fog, and coordination issues, unable to do much of anything for months. Overcoming the new physical and emotions challenges would be a big hurdle. Balaster needed to relearn how to learn because he lost many of his former abilities.

There was an uphill battle and the processed liquid hospital food was not helping. Luckily, Balaster was introduced to a new nutritional program. After starting the new dietary approach, the brain fog began to dissipate. This newfound clarity prompted Balaster to dive deeper into the world of nutrition, searching desperately for information to help his brain recover.

Balaster developed a nutritional plan of what to eat liberally and what to reduce or remove entirely. Water, colorful fruits and vegetables, bone broth, healthy fats like olive oil, and some protein from fatty fish and animals. Eating good foods wasn't enough, Balaster needed to stop consuming foods that were getting in the way of his recovery progress. He reduced his consumption of processed foods, refined sugars, vegetable oils, artificial sweeteners, foods with trans fat, and a number of grains.

The research and dietary changes worked. Balaster recovered so well he now can drive, play guitar, and even do back flips off diving boards.

Food has the power to save lives. Food can transform our mind.

***

Yet, why should food only be important for one of our brains when we have two? Okay, we don't actually have two brains, but we do have a system of neurons that stretches across our digestive tract called the *enteric nervous system*. This system contains the second largest network of neurons in our body and can operate independently of the brain. Thus, the gut has become known as the "second brain."

We find about 95% of our serotonin, the hormone that is involved in almost everything, including appetite, sleep, and memory, in our gut. We also find about 70% of our melatonin in the gut.

There are also trillions of bacteria, fungi, and other microbes hanging out in our digestive system. Collectively, they are all part of our *microbiome.*

This means the food we eat isn't just for us, it's for our gut bacteria. They help us digest food, absorb nutrients, provide energy, fight off bad bacteria, and regulate our immune system.

Our gut is a direct connection to our brain. The food we eat directly influences how we think and feel. Think about how you felt after eating way too much candy and compare that to a healthy home-cooked meal.

The field of nutrition science is evolving into a world of personalization. Nutrients are studied together because we rarely eat one in isolation.

We each have unique backgrounds, including our: culture, climate, past diets, age, stress level, gender, ethnic heritage, hormones, genetics, sleep, smoking, addictions, alcohol, physical activity, mental health, traumas, and food preferences. It is unrealistic to expect a nutrition finding can be applied in the exact same way to a diverse group of people.

The most important thing to remember when it comes to nutrition and diet is to explore and find what works best for you.

BRAIN FOOD

While it is important to understand the nutrients in our food, we don't eat nutrients; we eat food.

The following foods can have a big impact on our brainpower. Foods work together, so incorporating a variety will yield the best results.

Here are some key takeaways for choosing our brain foods:

- Prioritize whole, minimally processed foods over processed foods. Think water, steak, potatoes, and green beans vs. frozen pizza and candy bars.
- Strive for a colorful plate. The more colors, the greater variety of micronutrients.
- Food is neither "good" nor "bad." We don't need every meal to be "brain optimal." Before deciding on what to eat, we can ask "what would be a little bit better than this?" and then make a choice that aligns with our goals.
- Nutrition is personal. Finding what foods work best for us is an experiment. We can try new foods, see how we

feel, and then make a decision if we want to include it in our diet.

WATER

Our body is 60% water and our brain is 73% water. Water is essential to life, which is why we can only survive 4-7 days without water. We need water to produce hormones and neurotransmitters, help cells to grow, flush waste, transport oxygen, protect our brain, and so much more.

It's no wonder why dehydration has so many detrimental effects – from difficulty paying attention to memory impairment. Researchers have found that our performance on attention related tasks declines as we become more dehydrated. MRI scans even show that our brain can shrink when it becomes dehydrated.

Decreasing our water intake by just 3-4% can immediately negatively affect our brain, causing brain fog, fatigue, reduced energy, and mood swings. Even a 1-2% drop in body weight from fluid loss can bring on the headaches and decrease our mental performance.

The best way to tell how much water to drink is to drink until we aren't thirsty anymore. There is no need to keep chugging water if our body isn't telling us it needs more.

THE PLANTS

Leafy greens – Low in sugar and packed with vitamins, minerals, phytonutrients, and anti-inflammatory carotenoids, these vegetables are a staple for our brain. Examples of leafy greens include kale, spinach, arugula, cabbage, mustard greens, and romaine lettuce. A 2017 study found that consuming leafy greens was associated with keeping our brain looking younger, 11 years in fact!

One particularly brain boosting compound found in leafy green is the macromineral magnesium. Macromineral meaning we need to consume a large amount for optimal health. Magnesium helps hundreds of enzymes in our body do their jobs, from generating energy to DNA repair. Magnesium is found in chlorophyll, the molecule that makes plants look green, making leafy greens an excellent source.

Sea Veggies – Yes, even the ocean is rich in vegetables. While most commonly found in Asian foods, seaweed is a rich source of bioactive compounds not found in land plants and has a list of vitamins and minerals a mile long.

Sea vegetables are particularly rich in iodine, which plays a role in our metabolism. Sea vegetables are also good for muscle growth and can protect us from toxins and heavy metals. Sea vegetables come in a variety of colors (algae, red, brown, green) so we have plenty of options to mix and match.

You can find these in grocery stores and online either as whole food, flakes, powders, or supplements. A good place to start would be alternating between kelp and dulse supplements in capsule form.

Dandelions – A staple of the Mediterranean diet, these greens have quite a number of brain boosting effects. They are full of nutrients like vitamin B6, C, E, and K, including folate, choline, beta-carotene, minerals, and fiber to boot.

Sulfur Rich – Cruciferous vegetables, which include broccoli, cauliflower, cabbage, and Brussels sprouts, are a source of *sulforaphane*. Neither a vitamin nor a mineral, sulforaphane is a genetic modulator that helps activate an antioxidant pathway responsible for cleaning up oxidative stress.

Wait, there're more sulfur rich vegetables to choose from including: garlic, onions, turnips, radishes, and mushrooms. These vegetables support the health of our blood vessels, including the 400 miles of them in our brain. Healthy blood vessels promote better blood flow, which helps circulate nutrients throughout our body. If this process is running sub-optimally our brain is not only deprived of nutrients, leftover waste in our brain is staying put.

Garlic, onions, chives, leeks, and shallots (allium vegetables) pack a powerful punch. Garlic may reduce the risk of dementia by scavenging oxidants, lowering blood pressure, and protecting our neurons. Another added bonus is that garlic supplementation is able to reduce the length of our colds vs. a placebo, reducing sick days from 5 to 1.5 in total. It's hard to be at our mental best with a cold bringing us down.

Another source of sulfur and B vitamins are mushrooms. Not everyone reacts well to mushrooms, so if you notice effects like fatigue or brain fog, stop eating them at least temporarily. There are a wide range of mushrooms to choose from including button, Portobello, shiitake, crimini, oyster, and reishi. Be a little adventurous and find something that you enjoy – there is even mushroom coffee.

OMEGA 3'S & MCT OIL

Omega 3 fatty acids are great for our brain health, providing almost a protective shield for our brain and even helping it to recover from damage. Two major types of omega 3's are *docosahexaenoic acid* (DHA) and *eicosapentaenoic acid* (EPA).

Good sources of omega 3's include fatty fish like salmon, algae, krill & fish oil, grass-fed and finished beef, chia seeds, flax seeds, sacha inchi seeds, and pasture raised eggs.

When supplementing with fish oil, make sure the oil has a high proportion of EPA and DHA. Examine.com recommends supplementing between 250-1000 mg per day, best when taken with meals.

Another fatty acid with brain boosting benefits is MCT oil (medium chain triglycerides). MCTs are commonly found in coconut oil and have been shown to boost cognition, improve memory, and even give us extra energy. Studies have shown MCT oil enhances the effects of DHA and EPA omega fats when paired together.

MCT oil is often mixed in coffee. An emulsified version mixes better than a regular version because oil and water don't like to mix. Begin slowly when adding in MCT oil to your diet since too much could cause stomach issues. 1 tsp is a good starting point.

FRUITS

It is time for some sweets, nature's sweets that is. Fruits are full of sugar, but they also contain healthy amounts of fiber, which gives it a solid structure. The sugar from fruit does not just rush straight into our bloodstream; the fiber slows down the absorption, resulting in a longer release period.

Without fat or fiber, sugar will race into our body. Watch out for sugar-sweetened beverages, especially those with fruc-tose, as it cannot be used in other bodily functions right away. Fructose can impair its own absorption and that excess fructose can cause issues in our gut. Look at the nutrition label of a carton of orange juice and compare it to the back of a bottle of pop, you will probably be surprised by just how much sugar is inside.

Avocados – This super food is packed with nutrients and is one of the most calorie dense foods out there. This fruit, actually a single seed berry, is full of brain powering mono-unsaturated fats. Avocados are rich in fiber with about 12 grams in one fruit. They are a good source for our vitamin E needs, contain carotenoids, lutein, and zeaxanthin, and have twice the amount of potassium as a banana.

Blueberries – One of my favorite fruits is the tiny blueberry. It is full of antioxidants and flavonoids, polyphenol compounds (micronutrients). The darker the pigment of fruit, the more antioxidants it has. Blueberries have been shown to boost mood and improve memory function, supporting brain signaling and spatial working memory, thanks to a helpful flavonoids called *anthocyanins.*

Kiwi – With twice the amount of vitamin C as oranges and more fiber than oranges, apples, bananas, strawberries, and blueberries, this fruit may need a spot in your daily routine. The magic of the kiwi fruit not only helps with digestion, it also has been to shown to improve sleep onset, duration, and quality when eaten before bed.

EVOO – Extra-virgin olive oil or EVOO is here in the fruit section, because... olives are fruit. Commonly found in Mediterranean diets and delicious when paired with some good bread, EVOO has been shown to protect our brain and in some cases, improve cognitive function. It also helps to fight off amyloidal plaques by supporting the enzymes that break down the plaque. EVOO is also a great source for monounsaturated fats and vitamin E, just like avocados.

Cacao – Sweet, sweet chocolate. Yes, chocolate comes from berries and has brain boosting benefits, bringing antioxidants like theobromine and compounds like caffeine to boot, but before you go reaching for that king-size Hershey's bar, there is a certain type of chocolate that supplies these benefits.

Cocoa flavanols found in chocolate have been shown to improve blood flow to our brain, boost athletic performance, and slow cognitive aging. A longitudinal study published in 2016 found that people who ate chocolate a minimum of once per week had better working memory, abstract thinking, and visual-spatial memory.

Clinical trials showed that cocoa drinks full of flavonoids improved attention and memory in eight weeks. Max

Lugavere, author of *Genius Foods*, recommends looking for dark chocolate bars with cacao content over 80% and to avoid chocolate that has been Dutch processed, which takes healthy nutrients and degrades them so they turn into empty calories.

FERMENTED

Cultured or fermented foods have been around for thousands of years. They are rich source of probiotics (healthy gut bacteria), which help with digestion. Examples include kombucha, kimchi, sauerkraut, and yogurt. The probiotic goodness found in fermented foods has even been shown to help with anxiety. A study performed by the University of Maryland and the College of William and Mary found that the probiotics changed the gut environment, which in turn had a favorable influence on anxiety.

When looking for a good source of fermented foods make sure to check the refrigerated section as they will likely still have their good bacteria. Avoid fermented foods on the shelf because they will likely have been pasteurized which kills off the beneficial bacteria.

THE MEATS

You might be thinking that meat sources are only good for protein, but they bring a host of other benefits as well.

In his book *Genius Foods*, Max Lugavere explains that grass-fed beef contains nutrients and minerals like iron, zinc, omega-3's, vitamin B12, vitamin E, and creatine. Charlotte Neumann, a researcher at UCLA found that children consuming meat were healthier and had better cognitive function than other children.

Two less traditional foods in this category include organ meats and bone broth (AKA stock). The big benefit here comes from collagen and its amino acids. One of these aminos is glycine, which can give our brain a boost in serotonin and even improve sleep quality.

Organ meats are also full of nutrients like vitamins (A, B, D, E, & K), coenzyme Q10 (helping convert food into energy), and nutrients helpful for synaptogenesis like DHA, uridine, and choline. While we can prepare these like any other meat, we can also find them in supplement form.

Bone broth is like soup, full of healthy minerals that enable our body to function optimally. A South American proverb even said, "Good broth will resurrect the dead."

The big brain wins from bone broth come from glycine, which stimulates the production of glutathione. This is the "master antioxidant," which acts as a detoxifier. The more glutathione the better as this detoxification agent helps lower oxidative stress, eliminate heavy metals like mercury and lead, and better absorb nutrients.

Then there is glucosamine, which serves as our inflammation fighter. Glucosamine works to counteract the toxic effects on inflammation on our brain from things like oxidative stress or toxins from our diet, like alcohol.

NOOTROPICS

Nootropics, sometimes called smart drugs, are a collection of supplements, herbs, and compounds, which enhance brain function.

Often included in this group, coffee (caffeine) is probably the most the most widely used nootropic in the world. Some nootropics provide instant effects, while others work more like vitamins for our brain.

The supplementation industry is massive and unfortunately, not every company has our best interests in mind. There is often a gap between what companies will promise and what we actually experience.

I always recommend doing some research of your own before going out to buy any new product. Searching for an ingredient

---

on Examine.com or the National Institutes of Health (NIH) dietary supplements page is a great place to start.

With any new supplements start slowly, with low doses, to see how your body responds before upping the amount. Play it safe and check with your doctor beforetaking new supplements, especially if you have any medical conditions or are currently taking any medications.

A supplement guide can be found at the end of this book.

SLEEP

"Sleep is the single most effective thing we can do to reset our brain and body health each day." – Mathew Walker, *Why We Sleep: Unlocking the Power of Sleep and Dreams*

Our body has a dynamic, self-setting, 24-hour master clock inside which controls our hunger, thirst, and tells us when to wake up and when to go to sleep. This master clock is commonly known as our *circadian rhythm*.

Our body likes light. Sunlight exposure helps us wake up by sending signals that release daytime hormones and neurotransmitters. Our eyes take in light and let our brain know it should produce serotonin, which helps regulate attention during the day.

Traditionally our circadian rhythm follows the rising and setting of the sun, remaining in sync with the environment. However, our body has been thrown for a loop by the modern day schedule

With limited sunlight exposure during the day and artificial light in the evening, our biological clock is left wondering whether it is time for bed or time to get up. That's why is it is easy to feel tired during the day and awake at night.

Light exposure is great in the morning, but it can be a problem at night. At night, serotonin is converted into melatonin, which helps us fall asleep. However, light exposure at night prevents melatonin production, disrupting our circadian rhythm and making it more difficult to sleep.

Getting our master clock in line is the starting point for a good night's sleep and a healthy brain.

WHY WE SLEEP

We know sleep is good for us, but we don't fully understand exactly why we sleep.

There are few key reasons why scientists think we sleep:

- Sleep improves learning and memory
- Sleep removes toxins in your brain
- Sleep promotes recovery and optimal body function

When we sleep, our brain does not shut down. Our mind is still active, processing information from the day. Sleep gives our brain time to hard wire things we learn during the day. Our brain consolidates information and reinforces our neural connections, which form memories during sleep.

During the day, our brain and billions of cells are busy working. They do a lot of good work, but like any work environment, there is going to be waste left over.

Our brain needs regular cleaning to keep things in tip-top shape. A special cleaning system called the *glymphatic system* comes out at night to clear out toxins, dead cells, waste protein like amyloid-beta, and other leftover waste. This system is controlled by glial cells and uses a special fluid to flush out built up waste.

Our body also needs time to rest and repair. Sleep is an opportunity for our cells to recharge so we can wake up with a clear mind.

THE SLEEP DEPRIVATION PROBLEM

Sleep deprivation makes us dumber.

After 24 hours of sleep deprivation 6% less glucose (energy) reaches our brain. This is a problem.

However, the big problem is not simply the reduction in glucose to our brain; it is *where* the reduction takes place. Our parietal lobe and prefrontal cortex lose between 12 to 14% of their glucose – not good news since these areas are responsible for our high order thinking: social control, distinguishing between ideas, and determining the difference between good and bad.

That's not all. Sleep deprivation is the psychological equivalent of being drunk or high.

A study published in the American Academy of Sleep Medicine reviewed the top causes determining poor academic performance and found that poor sleep was equivalent to binge drinking and marijuana use. Dr. Charles Czeisler, Professor of Sleep Medicine at Harvard Medical School adds, "We now know that 24 hours without sleep or a week of sleeping four or five hours a night induces an impairment equivalent to a blood alcohol level of .1%. We would never say, 'This person is a great worker! He's drunk all the time!' yet we continue to celebrate people who sacrifice sleep for work."

Sleep deprivation is an ongoing problem and it has only been getting worse. In 1942, Americans were averaging 7.9 hours of sleep, with 84% getting 7 or more hours. As of 2013 Americans are now averaging only 6.8 hours.

YOUR SLEEP STRATEGY

Sleeping is a skill you can improve. Everyone should be able to get a good night's sleep. Here are four tips you can follow to get a better night's sleep and have a well-rested mind.

Black It Out

- When it is time for sleep, light is not your friend. Researchers at Cornell University studied how light impacts sleep. They put a tiny light behind the knee of a test subject during sleep, in an otherwise completely dark room. Despite complete darkness, the tiny light negatively impacted body temperature and melatonin secretion, worsening sleep quality. Imagine what even more light would do to your sleep.
- Action item: Cover your windows with blackout curtains, tape over the lights on your electronics, and remove the bright clock sitting next to your nightstand. Remove as much light as possible from your sleep sanctuary.

Caffeine Curfew

- Caffeine is great. It makes you feel less tired when you need a boost of mental energy. However, it doesn't just disappear when you are ready for bed. Caffeine has a half life of 6 hours so it takes a while to work its way through your body. Researchers found that consuming caffeine up to 6 hours before bed can cause disruptions during the night and reduce sleep time by an hour.
- Instead of hitting snooze to get a couple extra minutes, avoid caffeine in the 6 hours before going to bed to get an extra hour of quality sleep.

Power Down

- In the early 1900s this probably wasn't a big problem, but in our world today, we constantly face this challenge: addiction to technology. Blue light from our devices signals to our brain that it is daytime. Research has also shown that these devices can leave you wired after using them, leaving your mind engaged instead of ready for sleep. Alerts during the night from your phone can also disturb your sleep.
- Turn off the TV, shut your laptop, and put your phone down for 30 minutes for bed. At least dim the brightness and turn on nighttime mode. This helps limit the effects of blue light.

Money Time

- Between 10 p.m. and 2 a.m. is money time for sleep. "Around 10:00 p.m., your body goes through a transformation following the natural rise in melatonin. The purpose of this transformation is to increase internal metabolic energy to repair, strengthen, and rejuvenate your body," explained sleep expert Shawn Stevenson. During money time sleep your body secretes higher doses of melatonin and human growth hormone (HGH), responsible for repair and restoration. Neurologist Kulreet Chaudhary, MD explained, "If your body is chronically deprived of the regenerative sleep between 10p.m.-2a.m., then you may still feel fatigued when you wake up in the morning."
- If your schedule allows, aim to be in bed from 10 p.m. – 2 a.m. to get amplified sleep benefits. At minimum try to get most of your sleep in when the sun is down.

Sleeping Only

- We want our bedroom to be an environment for sleeping. The Division of Sleep Medicine at Harvard explained, "Keeping computers, TVs, and work materials out of the room will strengthen the mental association between your bedroom and sleep."
- Keep the work and technology out, reserve your bedroom for sleeping only. This will help your brain build an association between your bedroom and sleeping, making falling asleep easier.

MOVE

"Exercise is the single most powerful tool you have to optimize your brain function." – John J. Ratey, MD

Exercise primes our brain for optimal learning. It helps us learn new information faster and supports memory creation. Exercise also improves brain function by supporting the growth and connection of neurons.

In the book *Spark: The Revolutionary New Science of Exercise and the Brain*, John Ratey, MD explains how exercise improves learning: "First, it optimizes your mind-set to improve alertness, attention, and motivation; second, it prepares and encourages nerve cells to bind to one another, which is the cellular basis for logging new information; and third, it spurs the development of new nerve cells from stem cells in the hippocampus."

Translation:

- Exercise helps you pay better attention
- Exercise helps you remember new information
- Exercise helps your brain produce new brain cells

***

Remember – neurons that fire together, wire together.

This idea is called Hebbian plasticity. "When we exercise, particularly if the exercise requires complex motor movement, we're also exercising the areas of the brain involved in the full suite of cognitive functions. We're causing the brain to fire signals along the same network of cells, which solidifies their connections," explained Ratey.

The cool thing about this is it enables us to learn better and it also means we can learn faster. Ratey added, "In a 2007 study, German researchers found that people learn vocabulary words 20 percent faster following exercise..."

Exercise is not just for our body, it supercharges our brain!

EXERCISE FOR YOUR BRAIN

There isn't an ideal type of exercise for building your brain, but each type is beneficial.

Complex activities and aerobic exercise are especially good for improving skill acquisition.

Ratey explained, "While aerobic exercise elevates neurotransmitters, creates new blood vessels that pipe in growth factors, and spawns new cells, complex activities put all that material to use by strengthening and expanding networks."

Combining aerobic exercise with complex, brain-challenging activity, like skiing or tennis, will yield significant learning benefits.

With exercise, like any new motor skill, we oftentimes feel and look a little awkward the first time we attempt it. I remember the first time I went to the gym. I was trying to bench a pair of dumbbells. My arms shook uncontrollably and my movements were jerky and awkward.

The more you practice the movement, the better you get at it because you are improving the neural connectivity of those pathways. "With the repetition, you're also creating thicker myelin around the nerve fibers, which improves the quality and the speed of the signals, and in turn, the circuit's efficiency," explained Ratey.

While the new exercise you are trying might feel awkward in the beginning, your brain is working overtime to help you solidify those connections and become a master.

*⁕⁕

We don't need a fancy training regimen to benefit our brain.

A walk will do.

Researchers at the University of Illinois at Urbana-Champaign studied the effect of exercise on cognitive control for academic performance. Students were split into two groups, with one group sitting still for 20 minutes, while the other group went for a walk.

After 20 minutes, each set of students completed cognitive and academic testing. The group of walkers performed significantly better than the students who sat still. MRI scans showed higher levels of brain activity in the walkers.

Something as simple as a walk has the power to wake up our brain and improve our mental performance!

Opportunities to add more walking are everywhere. You could take the stairs instead of the elevator, park farther away from the door, use a walking treadmill at work, walk to class instead of taking the bus, or walk your dog. Wearable devices that track your steps can also provide a boost of motivation. There are plenty of ways to walk more, think about how you could add some more walking in your life, and try it out.

Esports is a mental game. Professional gamers put in hours of practice to keep their minds sharp, but practicing isn't the only thing players do to train their minds.

The best Esports athletes in the world prioritize physical health to maintain peak mental performance.

Rick Fox is an NBA champion and owner of the professional Esports organization Echo Fox. Fox realized the importance of fitness to the health and mental performance of his team, which is why Echo Fox partnered with TriFitLA – a fitness club and USA Triathlon Certified Performance Center based in Santa Monica.

TriFitLA co-founder Gine Baski explained they partnered with the UCLA Brain Research Institute "to put together a baseline of cognitive factors" to test. These factors including blood pressure, body fat, VO2 max (how well our body consumes oxygen), working memory, reaction time, and grip strength (a measure of brain activity). Baski has the players monitor sleep and nutrition, as well as perform cardio, resistance training, meditation, and yoga.

The team at TriFit had to look beyond standard training practices and focus on the impact to cognitive factors with the Echo Fox players. "Beyond just the training, because it is a highly cognitive sport, we have to look at those indicators and what is going to move the needle the most on them: Is it the exercise, is it the sleep, is it nutrition, is it hydration?" explained Baski.

They found players improved 3-6% across the baseline cognitive factors.

***

Esports organizations are hiring trainers to help players manage the physical and mental stressors, which come with professional competition. From an outside perspective, gamers might look like they are not really doing much, but Esports personal trainer and founder of Esports Trainer, LLC, Jake Middleton explains this isn't the case. "At these intense competitions there is a huge toll being put on their bodies, physically and mentally."

Middleton explained teams have, "focused periods of training where they play for three hours, scrim against a team, and then take a small break. Then they go back to play for another focused three hours. After that they will exercise, eat healthy foods, go over film, and socialize."

Professor Ingo Froböse of the German Sports University in Cologne has been studying Esports athletes since 2011 and has also found Esports places a toll on athletes.

"We were particularly impressed by both the demands placed on the motor skills and their capabilities," Fröböse said. "The Esports athletes achieve up to 400 movements on the keyboard and the mouse per minute, four times as much as the average person...both hands are being moved at the same time and various parts of the brain are also being used at the same time," he added.

Middleton explained exercise directly improves gaming performance in three major ways:

1. Improved endurance – Players need to be able to remain focused through long matches.
2. An increased ability to cope with stress – High-pressure environments and demanding competition schedules can easily cause burnout in players.
3. Improved cognitive function – Gamers need to think clearly and quickly, processing information and making split second decisions.

Here are three exercises Middleton recommends for his Esports athletes:

1. **Body Weight Push Up** – This is a great compound exercise that works a number of upper body muscles.
2. **Body Weight Squat with Calf Raise** – This compound exercise works muscles in the lower body.

3. **Elbow Plank** – This exercise is great for improving core stability and strength.

Middleton recommends his Esports players perform these exercises before gaming sessions to prime themselves physically and mentally, as well as whenever they need a boost of energy. Workouts do not need to be overly complex to yield significant health benefits.

Esports professionals are placing great emphasis on physical health and overall well being to improve their mental performance. The same concepts can be applied to our studies or work. Our mind and body are connected: healthy body, healthy mind.

(A workout for improving brain function created by Middleton can be found in the appendix)

KEY TAKEAWAYS

- Nutrition is personal. Explore what works best for you. Try new foods and see how your body reacts and how you feel.
- Sleep is time for our brain to process the events of the day and reset. Build a sleep sanctuary and routine to get optimal sleep. You do not have to do everything at once,

but start with something simple like ordering blackout curtains.

- If the benefits of exercise could be sold in a pill, it would be the most prescribed drug in the world. Exercise optimizes brain function. We don't need to go to the gym seven days a week to get the benefits. A simple 20 – minute walk is enough to wake our brain up and improve cognitive performance.

6

ESCAPE THE MATRIX
MINDSET

———

"There is nothing either good or bad, but thinking makes it so."

– WILLIAM SHAKESPEARE

"Have you ever heard David Foster Wallace's commencement speech, *This is Water*?" I asked.

My friend replied he hadn't.

Wallace was an American writer and professor. His speech contained an important truth I knew we needed to cover. "Let me tell you a story about two fish," I said.

"There are these two young fish swimming along and they happen to meet an older fish swimming the other way, who nods at them and says 'Morning, boys. How's the water?' And the two young fish swim on for a bit, and then eventually one of them looks over at the other and goes 'What the hell is water?'"

The most obvious and important realities are often the hardest to see and talk about.

We are just like the two young fish. Our mindset is so ingrained in who we are, we don't even notice it.

Our mindset is water.

Once we become aware of the water, we can change everything.

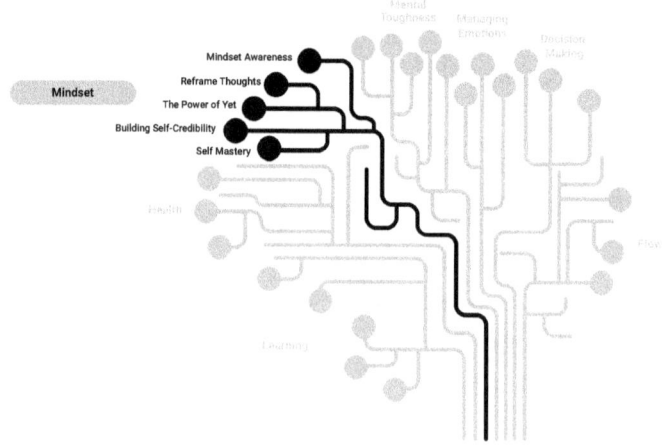

WHAT IS MINDSET?

On May 6, 1954, Roger Bannister broke the 4-minute mile barrier with a time of 3:59.4. On that day, Bannister showed the world what everyone thought was impossible was indeed possible. However, the biggest obstacle he had to overcome was not physical – it was mental.

British journalist and runner John Bryant provides a thoughtful reminder that world-class runners and coaches had been attempting to break the 4-minute barrier since 1886. He explains, "For years milers had been striving against the clock, but the elusive four minutes had always beaten them. It had become as much a psychological barrier as a physical one. And like an unconquerable mountain, the closer it was approached, the more daunting it seemed."

To run a mile under 4 minutes, Bannister needed the right mindset. Sure, speed and stamina were essential, but there were plenty of other great runners out there who physically could have completed the task. Those runners lacked the right mindset.

Bannister did not subscribe to the mindset the 4-minute mile could not be done. He chose to believe it was possible. This allowed him to take an "unreachable" goal and make it reachable.

While breaking the 4-minute mile barrier was an amazing feat, the effect Bannister had on others was just as astounding. Just 46 days after he broke the barrier, Australian runner, John Landy, set a new record of 3 minutes 58 seconds. One year later, 3 runners in a single race broke the barrier. As of 2018, more than 1,400 runners, including high schoolers, have broken the 4-minute mile barrier.

Bannister showed the world what was possible and his mindset helped him do it.

What have you already written off as impossible for your life?

***

In the movie *The Matrix,* Neo is offered a choice; take the blue pill or the take the red pill. The blue pill offered Neo the easy way out, to stay in the Matrix and continue living in blissful ignorance. The red pill offered another choice: the truth. It would reveal the way the world really is. Neo was living in the Matrix and the red pill was his chance to escape. He took it.

Our mind is the Matrix. And we are living in it. When we take the red pill, we choose to become aware of our mindset so we can begin to rewire our mind.

If the Shakespeare quote I used to open this chapter is true, then belief itself is a construct. Believing something is either good or bad, makes it so. The beauty of this construct is that at any moment, we can choose to believe different about ourselves and as soon we change that belief, it comes true.

If you think you are dumb, you will act in accordance with that belief. If you believe you are incapable of learning new things, guess what? You probably won't learn anything new.

Our thoughts and beliefs power our mindset. They shape how we see the world and guide our behaviors.

Now you have a choice. What do you choose to believe?

Once you've made the choice to believe that you can change your mindset, you've taken the first step toward developing your mindset.

There are three core tenets to developing your mindset:

1. Reframing Your Thoughts
2. Developing Your Self-Confidence
3. Mastering Your Self

Developing a strong mindset takes time. There is no silver bullet, but you can use the information in the following sections to rewire your mind.

REFRAME YOUR THOUGHTS

Reframing is a tool we can use to help rewire our mind to focus on positive thoughts instead of negative ones. Wayne Dyer said, "If you change the way you look at things, the things you look at change."

There is a basic principle behind reframing: *Events and situations do not have inherent meaning; rather we assign meaning based on our interpretation.*

Clinical psychologist Alia Crum tested this in her study "Mind Over Milkshakes." Study participants were brought into a lab and each person was given either a dessert shake or a health shake.

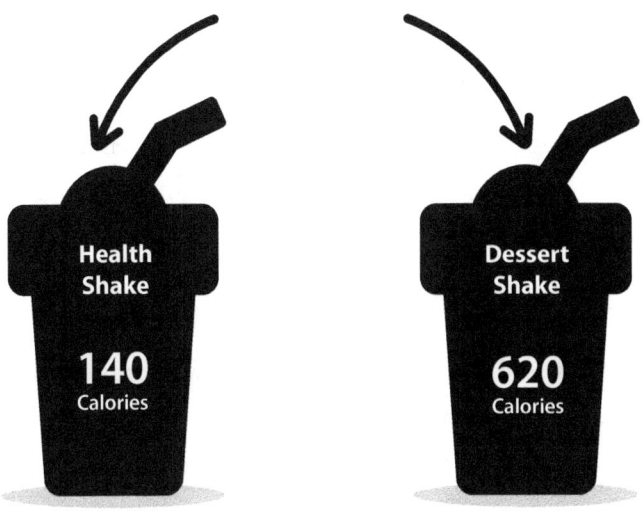

Actually both 300 calories

Health Shake
140 Calories

Dessert Shake
620 Calories

The group that drank the dessert shake saw their hunger hormone grehlin drop significantly, making them feel more full. The health shake group also saw grehlin drop, but not as much as the dessert group.

However, the shakes were identical. The only difference was the labeling.

Crum found, "Ghrelin levels dropped about three times more when people thought they were consuming the indulgent shake."

Our perception has power over our reality. Nothing is either good or bad until we assign it meaning, but we have the power to change that meaning.

Our thoughts dictate how we feel and act. When filled with negativity, we view our reality with a negative lens. Negative thoughts cause unnecessary stress and hold us back from our potential.

As discussed in chapter 1, there are two common mindsets: growth and fixed. We have the power to reframe our thoughts and choose what mindset we believe in.

The first step to reframing our thoughts is to become aware of our thoughts. Once we become aware, we can begin to replace our negative thoughts with positive ones.

Here are some examples of how to reframe your thoughts:

- Negative Thought: I am a failure.
- Positive Thought: I may have failed, but I can try again.
- Negative Thought: I always make bad choices.
- Positive Thought: There are positives and negatives with every choice.
- Negative Thought: I am worried about tomorrow.
- Positive Thought: What can I focus on right now?

Whenever you catch yourself thinking a negative thought, stop and think about how you can replace it with a positive one. Rewiring your thoughts will take time, but if you stick with it, the new thoughts can become hard wired in your mind.

USE THE MOST POWERFUL WORD

"I'm not good with names."

Have you ever said that before? I certainly have. However, I didn't realize I was actually less likely to remember someone's name when I kept saying, "I'm not good with names." It's an easy excuse, but we're not going to get any better if we keep telling ourselves the same story.

There is a powerful, yet simple way to reframe our thoughts. Anytime we catch ourselves saying "I am not good at XYZ" or "I can't," just add the word *yet*.

I am not good with names...yet. I can't get a job...yet. I am not in shape...yet. I haven't been able to win a championship...yet.

Add the word yet to any major or minor life goal you have, from going to college to landing a dream job. You will go from helpless and complaining to self-aware and optimistic.

Yet reframes the way we think. When you add the word *yet*, you give yourself permission to learn. When you don't add *yet*, you subconsciously acknowledge you are content with staying the same.

Yet is empowering. Not being able to do something is normal. When we are first learning to walk, we don't feel bad that we don't know how. We don't fall down and give up, we get back up and keep trying.

I haven't learned how...yet. I haven't worked hard enough... yet. I don't have the skills I need...yet.

The words "I can't" prevent us from trying anything new. By adding "yet," the entire meaning changes and we reframe our mindset around the challenge. We might not have the skills we need right now, but we have the capability to learn them.

Take stock of where you are and what you need to do to get where you want to go. Then go out and do it, so you can say "I can."

DEVELOP YOUR SELF-CONFIDENCE

Dr. Ivan Joseph, national champion soccer coach at Ryerson University, describes self-confidence as "the ability or the belief to believe in yourself, to accomplish any task, no matter the odds, no matter the difficulty, no matter the adversity."

Training our mind is just like training our body. Confidence is a skill we can learn and improve over time with practice.

The key elements to developing self-confidence include:

- Building Credibility With Yourself
- Choosing How You Interpret Feedback
- Visualizing Success

These elements build on each other. The more we master, the more confident we will become.

BUILD CREDIBILITY

Credibility builds confidence.

The key to earning credibility with ourselves is to do the work. Putting in time and effort to improve is the simplest way to build up our self-confidence.

The best way to feel more confident at the gym is to show up and workout. We will feel more confident giving a speech after we've practiced in front of our friend a few times. After we've dedicated the weekend to studying for our test on Monday, we will feel more confident.

My best advice for building credibility is this: if you commit to something and say you are going to do it, you follow through and do it, no excuses.

Developing self-confidence takes time and putting in hard work, especially when we don't feel like it.

***

While it is true that credibility builds confidence, the reverse is also true. "A confident and positive mindset can be both the cause of your actions and the result of them. The link between physical performance and mental attitude is a two-way street," explained James Clear.

Look to Russian chess grandmaster, world champion, and probably one of the greatest chess players ever to live, Garry Kasparov to see this in action.

In 1990, the World Chess Championship was set to begin. Garry Kasparov, the reigning world champion, was up against rival Anatoly Karpov. The two would play 24 matches over 3 months to determine who would be declared the winner.

Kasparov was known for his aggressive style of play and could intimidate his opponents. Another chess master commented, "Top grandmasters flinch under the tension of his style and confidence. You can tell from their moves they are scared. Their attacks are wild and hopeless or else very timid."

Kasparov started off well, but mistakes would soon creep into his play. After losing the seventh game and finishing the first 12 games tied with Karpov, Kasparov looked fragile. The *New York Times* reported, "Mr. Kasparov had lost confidence and grown nervous in New York."

Kasparov needed to turn things around if he wanted to maintain his championship status and prove he was still the best in the world for a reason. Kasparov had to rely on a mental game to conquer fear – act *as if* he were confident, in the hope of triggering the state.

Josh Waitzkin wrote in the *Art of Learning*, "Kasparov was an intimidator over the board. Everyone in the chess world was afraid of Garry and he fed on that reality. If Garry bristled at the chessboard, opponents would wither. So if Garry was feeling bad, but puffed up his chest, made aggressive moves, and appeared to be the manifestation of confidence itself, then opponents would become unsettled. Step by step, Garry would feed off his own chess moves, off the created position, and off his opponent's building fear, until soon enough the confidence would become real and Garry would be in flow. He was not being artificial. Garry was triggering his zone by playing Kasparov chess."

The mental game worked. By forcing himself to play aggressively, Kasparvov took the lead after the 16th match. He followed this up with two more victories in the 18th and 20th matches. When the dust settled, Kasparov retained his title of World Chess Champion, a title he would hold for another 10 years.

Kasparov acted *as if* he were confident, in order to feel confident and perform at his best.

You can do the same thing. Next time you find yourself scared by the thought of doing XYZ, imagine how someone doing it with confidence would look and act. Manifest that and try to imitate that; it will make you feel more confident as you go along.

Here are some examples of topics and the questions you can ask yourself to help you act more confidently.

- Health – What would a healthy person do?
- Studying – What would a top student do?
- Writing – What would a bestselling author do?
- Sports – What would a professional do?

Once you have an answer, you know what action to take. When you act confident and take action, you build credibility with yourself.

INTERPRET FEEDBACK

In the process of learning and earning credibility, we inevitably receive negative feedback.

Every time we receive feedback, we have a choice. We have the power to choose how we interpret the feedback. This is another key to self-confidence and it can go one of two ways.

1. We resist the feedback. We become demoralized and feel like a failure.
2. We accept the feedback with an open mind. We look for lessons to learn from so we can improve.

When we choose to interpret feedback in a way that serves us, it keeps us on the path toward self-confidence.

And drone racing is a perfect place to learn about this.

Jordan "Jet" Temkin is a drone racer. From a young age, he built and flew drones any chance he got. Racing drones is not a casual sport. Pilots wear VR Headsets, which feed into their drone's camera so they have a first person view. Using a remote control, these pilots get up to speeds of 100 mph, whipping around turns, and maneuvering past obstacles. It takes skill and coordination to be a pro drone racer and Temkin is one of the best in the world.

By 2016, Temkin was beginning to make a name for himself on the drone racing circuit. The Drone Racing League (DRL) approached him and asked him to compete in their league and inaugural championship. The DRL was an opportunity for Temkin to prove himself and he did just that, becoming the first ever drone racing champion.

As the second season of the DRL got underway, things did not go according to plan. After failing to place in the first few races of the season, Temkin was faced with a new set of challenges. There were new competitors, better racers, and mental hurdles that came with being champion.

Temkin had a choice: resist the feedback or accept it.

"I know from my previous background – I used to ski race when I was younger – when you have to prove something, or when you're trying too hard to beat a goal, it normally ends badly, just because you tend to over think," explained Temkin.

Temkin was stuck in his own head. His skills weren't as sharp as they needed to be and it showed. However, these setbacks were not going to stop him. Temkin knew the only way he would have a chance of coming back was if he faced the feedback and decided to do something about it.

Temkin started practicing even more, working on honing his skills and becoming a better pilot. This work paid off. Temkin bounced back and managed to pull off a podium finish in one of the final events of the year, securing an invitation to the season 2 DRL championship series.

In the beginning of the season, Temkin fell behind in the championship series standings, but through his refined piloting skills, strengthened mindset, and toughness in the face of adversity managed to make up ground and found himself trailing by a small margin going into the final race.

On the last loop of the last lap of the last race, Temkin took the lead and secured his second DRL championship.

Season 2 could have gone two different ways for Temkin. After the string of early failures, he could have gotten discouraged and quit, but he chose a different path. Temkin took the negative feedback in stride and chose to do something about it.

Every time you receive feedback, you have a choice of how you interpret it. It may sting and you may not like it, but how you respond matters. Learning to accept your failure is the first step to embracing a new challenge.

Feedback is an opportunity to improve. Fight the urge to resist the feedback and look for the lessons within.

VISUALIZE SUCCESS

"Been there, done that."

It's a simple phrase, but it holds an unexpected key to self-confidence.

As we gain experience, we gain confidence. When we know how to do something, we usually feel confident. But when we are about to do something where we lack experience like running a marathon, negotiating a raise, or going on a first date, fear can take over. Our brain struggles to make sense of the unknown.

However, there is a silver lining.

Research shows our brain is not good at differentiating between a real memory and an imagined one. When we vividly picture an image in our mind, our brain chemistry reacts as if it were a real memory.

Knowing this, we can use visualization to overcome fear and make the unknown known. If we can visualize a future event, our mind will think it is a real memory. Once it does that, it becomes something we've already experienced.

We will feel more confident in our abilities to go through that situation in the future because we've been there, done that (even if it is only in our mind).

However, in order for your visualization to be effective, it has to be believable.

Michael Gervais, sports psychologist, working with the Super Bowl champion Seattle Seahawks, prefers the word "imagery" to visualization because it entails the use of all our senses. He explains, "The objective is to create such a lifelike experience that your body believes that it could be real and it might just be."

When we picture this image in our mind repeatedly, our mind begins to believe it. It allows us to live in that future moment and plan for the challenges we may face.

Visualize success to conquer the unknown. To overcome fear and anxiety, imagine what a future situation will feel like as vividly as possible. Then you can say, 'been there, done that.'

MASTER YOUR SELF

"We think about self-esteem in one of two ways, either as the sole determinant of success or as the ultimate enemy," said Tom Bilyeu, founder of Quest Nutrition and Impact Theory.

Most people build their self-esteem around their accomplishments. You probably know some of them. They feel good about themselves if they make a lot of money, are the smartest person in the room, date the hottest person, get the best grades, have a nice house, or drive a new car. But there is a problem with this way of thinking.

Bilyeu explains, "When your ego is that attached to your success, it is devastated by your failures."

We need to stop placing our value in something, which depends on success or failure.

"If I pride myself on being smart and you tell me I'm dumb, and you put up a pretty good case for it, that's going to damage my self-esteem. My self-esteem in that situation is very fragile. If, on the other hand, you tell me that I'm dumb and

I build my self-esteem around being the learner, now I'm going to say thank you, please tell me in what way that I'm dumb because you will open my eyes to something that now I can address, and I can go learn about that thing and I will have a new skill," explain Bilyeu.

There is a subtle difference in this way of thinking. Nevertheless, the shift from being smart, to being the learner, makes all the difference.

There will always be someone smarter, stronger, or more talented than you are.

That doesn't matter. What matters is what you think about you.

Remember this: **What you build your self-esteem around matters.**

So build your self-esteem on what matters to you. Be a learner.

***

In the poem "Invictus," William Ernest Henley wrote, "I am the master of my fate; I am the captain of my soul."

We determine what our future brings. Where we are today is a byproduct of all the decisions we have made up to this moment.

We are in control of our life and it starts with what we think. Since our thoughts influence our actions, what we think matters.

One of the keys to mastering our self and developing a strong mind is the act of being self-compassionate.

Kristin Neff, University of Texas at Austin professor and author of *Self-Compassion* explained, "Self-compassion is not about a judgment or evaluation of self-worth; it's not about deciding whether or not we're a good or bad person; it's just about treating oneself kindly. Treating oneself like one would treat a good friend, with warmth and care and understanding... Self-compassion recognizes that it's natural and normal to fail and to make mistakes, and that we're worthy of kindness even though we've done something we regret or didn't perform as well as we wanted to."

At the end of the day, the only thing that matters is how you feel about yourself when you are by yourself.

One of the best ways to be more self-compassionate is positive self-talk. It even works for Navy SEALs.

Self-talk is one of four techniques the Navy uses to increase passing rates in the SEAL program. In a review of the documentary *The Brain*, Bakari Akil Ph.D. explains how this works, "The experts in *The Brain* documentary made the claim that we say 300 to 1000 words to ourselves a minute. By instructing the recruits to speak positively to themselves they could learn how to "override fears" resulting from the amygdala, a primal part of the brain that helps us deal with anxiety."

This addition helped increase passing rates from 25 to 33%.

If saying kind things to yourself is powerful enough to help soldiers get through some of the toughest training in the world, what could it do for your life?

FIND TIME FOR YOUR MIND

Our lives are busy. There is always something going on to grab our attention throughout the day. The first time we give our mind time to think is often when we are getting ready to sleep. The floodgates open and a million thoughts come rushing into our mind.

We rarely take time for our mind. It is hard to work on our mind when it feels like our thoughts are always focused somewhere else, often the past or future.

We need to find a way to bring our mind to the present moment. Being present helps us be more self-aware and make decisions with a clear mind.

Being present is a skill we can practice. One of the best ways to do this is meditation. Yes, meditation.

My friend Andrew Feinstein, author of *Find Your Mind: Meditation for the Bold and Ambitious*, likes to say meditation has a branding problem. The Zen art of meditation is not reserved for Buddhist monks, the enlightened among us, or the local yoga instructor.

"Meditation is a tool that places you in the present moment. It allows you to be fully present and let go of the things in your way," explained Feinstein. It is a useful tool to have in our mind training toolbox.

Meditation is not only useful for bringing ourselves to the present moment and tuning our distractions, but also helps strengthens our control over our mind.

Our mind is often running on autopilot and this can become a problem, especially when we come up against adversity. Our mind will opt for the path of least resistance, unless we tell it otherwise. We can't make the decisions we know will benefit us in the long term if our mind is off somewhere else.

Meditation gives us a tool to help us become aware of our self. With this awareness and ability to be present, we can shape our mind as we see fit. (There is a beginners' meditation included in the appendix at the end of the book)

MEDITATION SCIENCE DEEP DIVE

Meditation has science on its side. Studies show that meditation can physically change our brain. Consistent meditation helps forms new networks within our brain (neuroplasticity – Chapter 2).

Researchers from Johann Wolfgang Goethe-University & Brain Imaging Center looked at how meditation affects brain performance and attention, comparing three groups: older and long-time meditators, older with no meditation experience, and younger with no meditation experience. They found the older group of meditators outperformed non-meditators on attention assessments.

In 2005 Harvard's Sara Lazar, Ph.D. and her team studied meditators and non-meditators from the Boston area. They found meditators have thicker regions of gray matter in the brain, especially in the prefrontal cortex, the area responsible for working memory and executive decision making. In this particular region, the 50-year old meditators had the same amount of cortex as the 25-year olds. Meaning, meditation could help you prevent the breakdown of our brain associated with aging.

In a follow up 2011 study, Dr. Lazar took a group who had never meditated before and put them through an 8-week stress-reduction meditation-training program. Lazar measured their brains before and after the 8 weeks and found brain growth in the hippocampus, the area of your brain responsible for learning, memory, and emotion control, and the temporo-parietal junction, the area of your brain responsible for empathy, compassion, and perspective. They also found the amygdala, the fight-or-flight part of your brain, shrunk, and the degree to which it shrunk was correlated with the amount of stress reduction participants reported.

Yeah science!

KEY TAKEAWAYS

- The first step to transforming your mindset is to accept your current way of thinking needs an adjustment. If your current mindset is neither serving you nor helping you achieve your goals, it's time for a change.

- Reframing your thoughts can flip the switch from impossible to possible. Unshackle yourself from self-imposed limits to achieve your biggest goals.
- To build confidence, first build credibility with yourself. Put in the time and effort to get good at something, especially when you don't feel like it.
- Improve your self-compassion by practicing positive self-talk. Write down or say aloud one nice thing about yourself every day. If this is awkward or challenging, ask a close friend for help. They can sometimes see you better than you see yourself.
- Bring yourself into the present moment when you need to make key decisions. Your brain will run on autopilot unless you tell it otherwise. Sometimes you have to override that and make hard choices.

7

CALLUS YOUR MIND
MENTAL TOUGHNESS

———

"If you can't fly, then run, if you can't run, then walk, if you can't walk, then crawl, but whatever you do, you have to keep moving forward."

— MARTIN LUTHER KING, JR.

"Remember David Goggins?" I asked my friend.

"How could I possibly forget?"

"Whenever I have a choice between the easy way and the hard way, I think, 'What would Goggins do?' Then I go do that."

Building mental toughness is simple. Each time we choose to do something hard, over what is easy, we callus our mind.

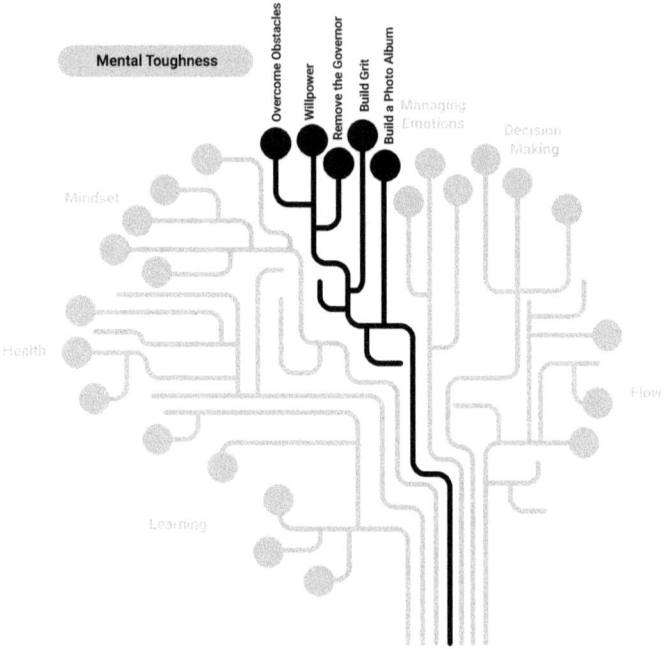

THE OBSTACLE IS THE WAY

"Men wanted for hazardous journey. Low wages, bitter cold, long hours of complete darkness. Safe return doubtful. Honor and recognition in event of success." – ad for the Endurance expedition.

In 1914 British explorer, Ernest Shackleton supposedly ran this ad in the London newspaper, *The Times*, for a harrowing journey to explore the Antarctic. While historians have been unable to find a copy of this ad, the message behind it rings true of a time "when ships were made of wood and men were made of steel." Ernest Shackleton was setting out for a Trans Antarctic expedition. On December 5, the crew left South Georgia, a small island in the south Atlantic.

It would be another 497 days before they touched land again.

In January 1915, The Endurance became trapped in ice. Shackleton and the crew hunkered down, distributed rations, created a routine of chores and found ways to stay entertained. Shackleton was respected by his men and looked to as a master of getting out of sticky situations.

The crew remained 1,200 miles from civilization and had spent seven months in the ship on the pack ice. However, in October the ice forced Shackleton and his crew to abandon the ship, setting up camp on top of the floating ice, their new home for the next six months. As they floated along on the ice floe toward Paulette Island, trying to reach a supply depot, they helplessly drifted past it.

On April 9, 1916, the ice floe began to break apart beneath their feet. Shackleton and the crew hurried onto their three small boats with a new heading of Elephant Island, 100 miles away. They battled raging storms for seven days, faced 17 hours of darkness each day, went days without sleep, and their mouths were so dry they could not swallow food. Eventually they made it to Elephant Island.

Realizing the crew had one hope of survival, Shackleton and a small crew of five men set off on the water again on a 23-foot boat, heading toward the whaling station on South Georgia Island, 800 miles away in search of help. The small crew again faced raging seas and extreme gales, with waves reaching heights of 50 feet. At one point Shackleton said, "I called to the other men that the sky was clearing, and then a moment later I realized that what I had seen was not a rift in the clouds but the white crest of an enormous wave." For 16 days, they made the journey despite perilous conditions. "Difficulties are just things to overcome, after all," said Shackleton.

They neared the south tip of South Georgia Island and as they finally broke through the ice into the bay and began pulling the boat ashore, the main pin holding the rudder fell out. Landing on the side of the island opposite the whaling station, they had to traverse glaciers and mountains never before traveled by man. With some rope and screws sticking out of their shoes for traction, Shackleton and two of the men set off without a map, leaving the other two behind, as they were too sick to continue. A few days later, three scraggly men made their way into the whaling station. Shackleton said, "Superhuman effort isn't worth a damn unless it achieves results."

It took three months, but in August 1916, Shackleton returned to Elephant Island to rescue what was left of his crew. Every single crewmember who set out on the expedition survived.

Despite setback after setback, Shackleton had the fortitude to push on, despite seemingly impossible odds. Others might have given up. Shackleton's story is one of adventure, leadership, suffering, and, like the rest of this chapter, mental toughness.

If you were in Shackleton's place, do you think you would have had the fortitude and mental toughness to survive? In this chapter, I will show you why superhuman mental toughness isn't as crazy as it sounds.

***

Marcus Aurelius once said, "The impediment to action advances action. What stands in the way becomes the way."

Hardship is inevitable. We can use challenge to our advantage. Each adversity is an opportunity to practice being our best self.

"Whatever we face, we have a choice: Will we be blocked by obstacles, or will we advance through and over them?" asks Ryan Holiday, author of *The Obstacle is the Way*. Learning to how to overcome obstacles makes us stronger.

Holiday gives us a framework for overcoming obstacles in daily life. He uses examples throughout history of great people who turned adversity into opportunity like Amelia Earhart, Alexander the Great, Theodore Roosevelt, and Steve Jobs.

The three elements for facing challenge are:

- Perception
- Action
- Will

"Our perceptions determine, to an incredibly large degree, what we are and are not capable of. In many ways, they determine reality itself. When we believe in the obstacle more than in the goal, which will inevitably triumph?" explained Holiday.

We must fight our gut reaction when it comes to obstacles. Instead of shying away from them and reacting emotionally, pause and look at the situation objectively. Once you do, you will realize it is not so bad. This change in perception turns the impossible into the possible. Once we see things as they truly are, we must do what we can.

When faced with an obstacle we can control how we respond. We must take disciplined action to overcome the obstacle. The solution might not be obvious, but through persistence and deliberate action, we can usually find a way.

In reality, some challenges are impossible to overcome. Here we must endure the hardship, strengthening ourselves to survive those hard times. As the stoics say, *sustine et abstine*, meaning bear and forbear. You can do two things: acknowledge the challenge and carry on anyway.

"You'll have far better luck toughening yourself up than you ever will trying to take the teeth out of a world that is—at best—indifferent to your existence," explained Holiday.

If you feel stuck by an obstacle start by imagining you are advising a friend. This helps us keep an objective view of the problem. The solutions to our friends' problems often seem obvious to us because we are not reacting emotionally.

We must practice the following maxims until they become hard-wired in our brain:

1. See things as they are
2. Do what we can
3. Endure what we must

We gather strength as we go. We need to put these into practice today; it is the first step to callusing our mind.

WILLPOWER

Part of being mentally tough is having the motivation and will to do hard things even when we don't want to. Motivation and willpower will not replace the habits and systems we need to build for long-term mental toughness, but they can give us the spark we need to head in the right direction.

There are two schools of thought when it comes to willpower:

1. We have a limited supply of willpower, meaning it can be depleted
2. We have an unlimited supply of willpower

While the first idea is more common, there have been studies on both ideas and each can help us strengthen our mind.

In the late 1990s at Case Western Reserve University, psychologist Roy Baumeister and his team came up with an experiment to test whether or not willpower could be depleted.

Cookies and radishes were provided for study participants to eat. One group was allowed to eat the cookies, but not the radishes, while the other group was the opposite. Each person was given an impossible puzzle to complete. The people who were not allowed to eat the cookies attempted the puzzle fewer times and gave up earlier than the group who was allowed to eat cookies, suggesting that they had used up their willpower earlier while resisting the cookies.

Saying no to temptations like candy or chocolate throughout the day can deplete our willpower. Taking initiative on a project or making plans takes energy and depletes our willpower. Even a long day of shopping, making decisions to buy or not to buy, depletes our willpower.

There is another side to the story though.

Carol Dweck and her team conducted a follow up study that confirmed willpower depletion is real, but also found that subjects who *believed* willpower was unlimited were able to overcome the effects of willpower depletion.

From the discussion, "Is just believing that willpower is not highly limited sufficient for successful self-control? Certainly not, but it may be an important ingredient... With a non-limited mindset and effective strategies, people may exert self-control over an extended period without frequent glucose boosts. As William James suggested more than a century ago, people have far greater capacity to exert self-control than they may believe."

∗∗∗

So how can we use these two ways of thinking to shape our lives?

First, I look to what idea will serve me the best. If we want to callus our mind, adopting the idea that willpower is unlimited can give us the mental edge we need to overcome challenges. With this mindset, I find I am less likely to make up excuses when I don't feel like doing something. It puts me in control of my life and my decisions.

However, I also like to take a practical approach. I like to shape my environment to help me avoid willpower drains. We are not going to make the hard decision every time, especially when we are busy or tired. The easier I can make difficult decisions, the ones I know are good for me, the better.

One of the best ways we can do this is by scheduling the most important things we have to do first. I go to the gym right after I wake up. That way I don't have any excuses later in the day in case I get busy or don't feel like it. I call this moving the big rocks. When we do this, regardless of what happens the rest of the day, we can feel good about getting something important done.

Here are some helpful ways you can use your will-power effectively:

- Set out your gym clothes the night before to make getting up and going to the gym easier in the morning
- Do your hardest task for the day first thing in the morning while you still have willpower
- Hide junk food (if you can't see it, you won't have to use willpower to constantly resist it)
- Put your phone away during work so you aren't tempted to check it.

Willpower depletion is real, but don't use it as an excuse for not doing something important. Willpower is a tool we can use to get us started, but building up habits and systems to tackle the hard things we have to do is the key to mental toughness. These systems not only save our willpower, they help us take on challenges and stick to our larger goals.

"Once you realize that willpower is just a matter of learning how to control your attention and thoughts, you can really begin to increase it."

THE CENTRAL GOVERNOR

In our cars there is device called a governor, which limits its top speed. This is installed as a protection mechanism for our safety.

Our brain also has a central governor to protect us. It keeps us safe, but also holds us back from pushing ourselves beyond our limits.

From a biological perspective, our brain wants to make sure we always have a little fuel left in the tank in case of emergency. While pushing our limits, 20 miles into a marathon our mind is saying we can't push any harder and our pace stays the same. "The brain regulates performance in anticipation to make sure that you don't harm your body," explained sports physiologist Tim Noakes.

However, as we round the final corner with the finish line in sight we can muster up enough energy to sprint toward the finish. Why? As we approach this finish line, our mind realizes that we can push harder and nothing bad will happen. We bypass the governor.

Noakes conducted an experiment with cyclists, attached wires to their legs, and asked them to cycle until exhaustion. As the cyclists neared exhaustion, their muscle fibers began to switch off and they said they were too tired to continue.

However, Noakes found the cyclists only activated about 50% of their muscle fibers when they couldn't pedal anymore. The riders were too tired to pedal, but they still had plenty of muscle available to keep going.

The brain was the limiting factor.

Our central governor is there to help protect us, but we are capable of more than our brain realizes at times. To grow, we must push past resistance and bypass the governor when we feel like giving up.

David Goggins created the 40% rule from his time in the Navy Seals. He said, "When you think that you are done you're only 40% in to what your body's capable of doing. That's just the limits that we put on ourselves."

We must remove the governor from our mind.

GRIT

If I could sum up grit in one sentence it would be, "I got this."

"I got this," says I am willing to put in the time and effort to achieve my goals. While talent and skill are important for achievement, without effort we won't get far.

Do you have grit? Are you willing to dedicate yourself to a major goal you have? If you don't feel gritty yet, that is okay. Grit is a skill we can develop over time.

Grit is defined as perseverance and passion for long-term goals.

Angela Duckworth is a psychologist and author of *Grit*. In her research on grit, Duckworth studied the relevance of grit in numerous groups including, West Point cadets, undergraduate students, and National Spelling Bee competitors. Strength did not predict which cadets passed brutal entrance tests, SAT scores did not predict GPAs of undergraduate students, and IQ did not predict performance in the spelling bee. Grit did.

Duckworth explained, "There are no shortcuts to excellence. Developing real expertise, figuring out really hard problems, it all takes time–longer than most people imagine...Grit is about working on something you care about so much that you're willing to stay loyal to it...it's doing what you love, but not just falling in love–staying in love."

To have grit means that we must remain resilient in the face of failure and maintain commitments toward our goals.

It does not matter how long it takes us to achieve our goals, we just have to keep putting one foot in front of the other.

Progress is progress, no matter how slow. Like Babe Ruth said, "You just can't beat the person who never gives up."

***

Grit does not just appear one day when we need it. We have to build it up.

Tim Grover trained some of the greatest basketball athletes of all time, including Michael Jordan, Kobe Bryant, and Dwayne Wade. Grover's players built up their grit through relentless training and practice. "My goal is to make it so challenging inside the gym that everything that happens outside the gym seems easy," explained Grover.

Mental toughness, like our body, is built up through small actions, repeated day after day. Every time we choose the hard path over the easy path, we build grit. Each time we do something hard, we develop the confidence and mental toughness needed to take on bigger obstacles.

I've found physical challenges to be one of the best ways to build up mental toughness. It is easier to grasp the idea of mental toughness when it is tied to something real. Every time I show up for a workout, I build up grit. Every time I push myself, even though I am tired, I become mentally stronger.

I believe that physical challenges can unlock the power of our mind. I discovered that the discipline it takes to show up at the gym and workout translates over to all areas of my life.

The gym was training ground to develop grit, but we can develop grit throughout our lives. It requires that we do the hard work. We need to prove to ourselves that we have the courage to do the hard things.

Here are some ways that you can train your grit and callus your mind:

- Do one more rep at the gym when you are ready to quit
- Study ten more minutes when you would rather be hanging out with friends
- Say no to a night out to study for a test
- Surround yourself with gritty people
- Work an extra hour to finish a project
- Ask another question if you are still confused
- Set your alarm and get out of bed without hitting snooze

Show up consistently and when you commit to something, follow through. It is that simple.

We can't fake mental toughness. We have to earn it.

YOUR PHOTO ALBUM

We can use past experiences to help us through new challenges. I call this building your photo album. Each hardship we face and challenge we overcome is added to the album. We can look back at all the successes and failures we've overcome to help us in times of doubt, serving as a reminder that we are capable of taking on great obstacles.

I did not run the World's Toughest Mudder (WTM) without preparing and building up my mental toughness. Each challenge I faced along the way callused my mind and prepared me for the journey ahead.

Long before running WTM even crossed my mind, I began building up experiences for my photo album.

I had been going to the gym consistently for a few years and was looking for a new challenge. I saw a few people running marathons and thought that would be a good place to start. Mind you, I had never run more than a 5k in my life. I had effectively no experience running at this point, but knew I needed to start somewhere.

Running your first marathon starts in training. It is not realistic to expect you to run 26.2 miles without building up to that. Each day you train leading up to the marathon is both physical and mental preparation.

Each week you run a little farther than the week before. This prepares your body to be able to handle the physical demands of running a marathon. But more importantly, it strengthens your mind. You begin to see what's possible. Once you've run five miles, six doesn't seem so bad. Each new challenge you overcome adds a picture to your album. When combined with the "one more" mentality, this helps push you beyond what you once thought was impossible.

Race day arrives and we have built up our photo album of all the training runs and hurdles we overcame to get to this day. Now it is time to add a highlight to the photo album. The marathon will push you to your physical and mental limits. It is a great one-time challenge to test yourself and see what you are capable of.

I had done everything I could to prepare for my race, the Sydney Marathon, but it was still a daunting obstacle. I hit the wall 18 miles in. I could barely pick up my legs to run. I began to question why I was even out running, but I kept moving forward. It had started to rain, but that was not going to stop me. My energy was drained and my strength sapped as I rounded the final corner. When the Opera House and the finish line came into view, I knew I had made it. Crossing the finish line brought on a surge of emotion. I had doubts along the way, but I did it. I finished my first marathon and added a new highlight to my photo album.

Completing the Sydney Marathon gave me confidence that I was capable of more than I realized. Despite questioning my ability through all the miles and wanting to give up on more than one occasion, I made it across the finish line. Maybe WTM wasn't a crazy idea after all. But I felt like I still needed more training.

I followed up my first marathon with my second eight months later at Grandma's Marathon in Duluth, MN. Two months later, I completed my first 50-mile trail ultramarathon, the Lake Superior Voyageur. One month later, I paced 37 miles of the Superior 100-mile trail race through the night. Each experience added to my photo album, preparing me for WTM.

Each obstacle you overcome is a memory in your photo album that you can look back on when you need to. You earned these memories and no one can ever take that away. Remember the highs and lows that come with each memory and use them to conquer the challenge ahead.

KEY TAKEAWAYS

- C.S. Lewis once said, "Hardships often prepare ordinary people for an extraordinary destiny." We must lean into the challenges we face to accomplish our biggest goals.

- Look at obstacles objectively. Put yourself in a friend's shoes and look at your problem from their lens. If that doesn't work, ask a friend for help.
- Overcome limited willpower by scheduling your most important things early in the day or by setting aside time in your calendar for these activities. Make your hardest tasks the easiest to do by removing barriers that suck up willpower.
- Train your grit through small actions like completing one more rep, studying for ten more minutes, and getting out of bed without hitting snooze. These small wins will build on each other and make grit come more naturally.
- Use past experiences as motivation to take on new obstacles. Keep a photo album in your mind, meaningful pictures on your phone, or keep a collection of objects like a marathon medal to look to when you need a reminder that you are strong and capable.
- Each time we stretch ourselves outside of our comfort zone we rewire our brain. Starting a new job is challenging, but over time we adapt and establish a new normal. The same applies to mental toughness.

8

APATHEIA
MANAGING EMOTIONS

"You have power over your mind – not outside events. Realize this, and you will find strength."

— MARCUS AURELIUS

"How did you handle all of the emotional highs and lows during the race?" asked my friend.

"I have another story to share with you that I think might help," I replied.

An ancient Persian king once called all his sages together and asked them for a saying that would be true at all times, in every situation, in every circumstance, and in every place.

The sages gathered and thought about the answer for a long time. After a lengthy discussion, one sage had a suggestion. The rest of the sages agreed and decided to tell the king.

The sages gave the king a ring with a simple engraving: *this too shall pass.*

This is the fundamental truth of emotion. Happiness comes and goes. Sadness comes and goes. Anger comes and goes.

No emotion lasts forever.

No matter how bad things may seem, take solace in this truth.

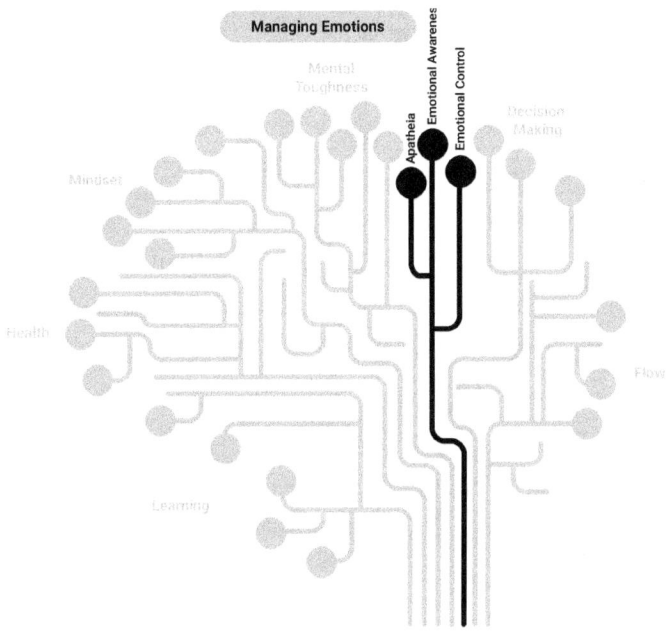

UNDERSTANDING EMOTIONS

Mental health and mindset can make you or break you.

Growing up I lived a comfortable life. I was shy and went through phases of social awkwardness (thank you grades 6 through 12), but things were good. While I had dreams of being Harry Potter or a big shot professional athlete, I was the quiet, reserved kid who did not speak up much. I never smiled showing my teeth and talking to girls was out of the realm of possibility – I was far too scared to do that.

Long before I saw any physical changes, a switch flipped in my mind. It wasn't until I gained confidence through weight lifting that I realized I had low self-esteem and social anxiety. It was like the fog cleared and for the first time I saw a world of possibility. I was more confident and stopped letting my perception of what others thought of me get in my head. I started smiling showing my teeth, and even mustered up the courage to talk to girls for the first time (holy awkward).

My life trajectory changed. I continued on that path and my confidence grew over the next few years. I went off to college and everything was good. Classes were going well, my workouts felt great, and I found a close-knit community to call home.

Midway through my fall semester of my sophomore year, I became lost. Changing friendships and self-imposed pressure to "have it all together" got to me.

My sense of purpose began to unravel and I became disillusioned with school. I was staring down the barrel of the "American Dream" – a nine-to-five desk job typing away at a computer, mindlessly staring at spreadsheets for the next forty years while life passed me by.

It drained my soul just to imagine it. This was going to be my life after college – meaningless, dull, and unhappy.

For the first time in my life, my mental state began to splinter. I no longer wanted to do the things I used to like and every day felt empty. I went to class, did my homework, and got a workout in even though I did not feel like doing anything. My willpower and inner identity kept me going.

I played games, hung out with friends on the weekend, and experienced moments of joy, but the dark cloud remained ever-present until two things happened, which turned my mental decline around.

On a career trek to visit local companies, I realized there were companies who shared my work values. They weren't all "work hard, play hard," but rather talked about how their work felt meaningful, solved problems, and made a difference.

The first switch was flipped. I realized there were places where I could actually see myself after graduation.

The second moment began as summer was approaching and I still did not have a job. Despite countless rejections, I decided to look through internship postings one more time to see if I could find one.

I stumbled upon one for a company called Meister MMA. I reached out to the owner, Cole Peyton, and got an interview. During the interview, I felt like I met another me. We had similar backgrounds and shared many of the same views on work and business. Cole worked in corporate America and used what he learned to launch his own business. He was forging his own path and I knew I wanted to spend time with him. A week after the interview I got a call from Cole informing me that I got the position. I was so excited that I think I said "I accept" before he even finished talking.

As I worked through the summer with Meister, my entire worldview changed. My eyes were opened to a new realm of possibility and it had a profound impact on my psyche. I had purpose again and I gained one of my best friends in the process. I stopped seeing the working world as this evil place, full of soulless corporations, and instead saw opportunities to create and build — a chance to make a difference in the world.

I changed the way I looked at things, and the things I looked at changed.

THE EMOTIONAL SPECTRUM

The key to managing our emotions is to understand them first.

Emotions are part of who we are. One moment we may feel happy and the next we feel sad. Our emotions and feelings change as the neurochemicals in our brain change.

We live on a spectrum of emotion, moving back and forth along it. Our emotional spectrum is similar to the inverted-U performance curve from Chapter 3.

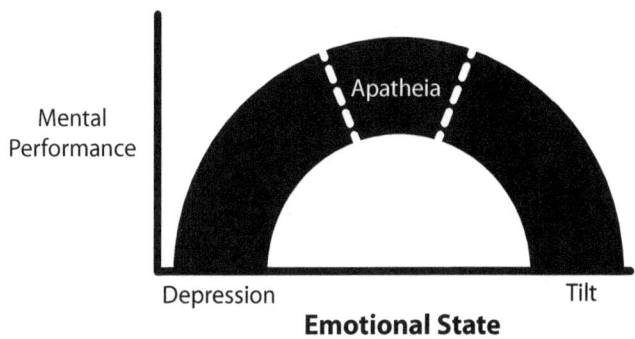

We can use this curve to help visualize how our emotions affect our mental performance. If we are too far to the left, we can experience depression, not feeling like doing much at all. If we move too far to the right, we can feel angry and lose control of our emotions, making poor decisions.

However, right in the middle is *apatheia*.

Apatheia is a Greek word, described by Stoics as "the kind of calm equanimity that comes with the absence of irrational or extreme emotions." Apatheia is a state of mental composure, a balanced mind, not the absence of emotions. Apatheia is not about pretending that our feelings don't exist, rather it is about learning to keep them in check.

We must monitor our emotions and learn to recognize where we are on the spectrum at any given time. As we find ourselves sliding to either end of the spectrum, we have a choice: a choice of how we respond.

Holocaust survivor and author of *Man's Search for Meaning*, Viktor Frankl explains, "Between stimulus and response there is a space. In that space is our power to choose our response. In our response lies our growth and our freedom." This belief helped Frankl survive multiple concentration camps, including Auschwitz.

As we work on managing our emotions, this belief will serve as a guiding principle.

UNDER EMOTING

"I began having suicidal thoughts as young as eleven."

Robert "Wobbles" Wright is a retired professional Esports *Super Smash Bros Melee* player who has spoken up about his personal mental health challenges. Wright became famous in the Melee community for his gameplay with the Ice Climbers character.

While his upbringing and family life was for the most part good, Wright was not. He needed an outlet, a distraction. That outlet became video games. "Video games were a great way for me to feel a shortcut to satisfaction. There is something incredible about video games' way of scaling, giving you a challenge you can defeat," explained Wright.

Gaming was not just a distraction; it became a way to build up his self-esteem and self-confidence. "When you're competing, it lights you up, it makes you present," he said. "Being able to be present is the antidote for depression. It says, 'Be awake, be here, right now. Play.'"

Wright is not the only Esports player to struggle with mental health. Long hours of training, alongside the stress and pressure of competition, can lead to mental health issues. Another Melee player, Justin "Plup" McGrath experienced a panic attack at the Evolution Championship Series. League of Legends pro, Diego "Quas" Ruiz spoke out about his struggles with depression after retiring from Esports.

Perfectionism, setting expectations too high, and making mistakes can lead to depression. Feeling like we are not enough in the eyes of those around us and fearing failure can also cause mental health challenges.

On the emotional spectrum, depression falls on the far left. When we are lacking motivation, we cannot operate at our best. While in a depressed state, we may struggle with cognitive tasks like concentration, learning, and decision making.

Depression has been linked to an imbalance of neurotransmitters in our brain, including serotonin, norepinephrine, and dopamine. These neurotransmitters help us regulate our bodies, respond to stress, and experience pleasure from seeking out rewards. While the neurochemistry and causes of depression are complex topics, low levels of these neurotransmitters can help explain some of what is happening in our brain during depressive states.

This understanding can help us look for solutions to overcome depression.

OVERCOMING DEPRESSION

Jane McGonigal, Ph.D. is a multiple time TED speaker and author of two books on how games change lives and make the world a better place.

In 2009, McGonigal's life went into a tailspin after suffering a debilitating concussion. "The concussion didn't heal properly, and after 30 days, I was left with symptoms like nonstop headaches, nausea, vertigo, memory loss, mental fog. My doctor told me that in order to heal my brain, I had to rest it. So I had to avoid everything that triggered my symptoms. For me that meant no reading, no writing, no video games, no work or email, no alcohol, no caffeine. In other words... no reason to live," recounted McGonigal.

McGonigal's doctor's guidance was not helping. She went into a dark place and started experiencing suicidal ideation. Thirty-four days after her concussion she gave herself an ultimatum – "I am either going to kill myself or I'm going to turn this into a game."

During games we "tackle tough challenges with more creativity, more determination, more optimism, and we're more likely to reach out to others for help," explained McGonigal. This realization led to the creation of what would eventually become the game SuperBetter.

SuperBetter is an online game designed to help build up personal resilience in the face of serious challenge, like depression, anxiety, or injury. Players complete challenges to help build up their four core resiliency strengths: physical, mental, emotional, and social.

After playing the game for just a couple of days, McGonigal noticed significant improvements in her health. She explained, "That fog of depression and anxiety went away. It just vanished. It felt like a miracle."

Since its creation, SuperBetter has helped more that 250,000 people overcome real life health issues like depression, anxiety, and brain injuries.

SuperBetter is based on the idea of *Post traumatic growth* (PTG). PTG is positive change which helps us appreciate our best qualities and lead a happier life after a traumatic experience or life struggle. What doesn't kill us, makes us stronger.

Here are some things people who experienced PTG tend to say:

- "My priorities have changed."
- "I'm not afraid to do what makes me happy."
- "I feel closer to my friends and family."
- "I understand myself better. I know who I really am now."
- "I have a new sense of meaning and purpose in my life."
- "I'm better able to focus on my goals and dreams."

Overcoming depression isn't easy, but there are some things that can help us re-center ourselves.

Exercise – In 2000, researchers at Duke compared the effectiveness of exercise vs. prescription drugs for the treatment of depression. The findings? Exercise is better than Zoloft for treating depression.

Research tested three groups: exercise, drugs, and exercise & drugs. All three groups showed lower levels of depression, with around half of each group in remission. However, six months after the study was completed the researchers followed up with the patients and found that exercise outperformed medicine over the long-term. The exercisers were more likely to stay out of depression in the long-term.

Antidepressants tend to help us feel physically better first, while we feel better about ourselves later. However, exercise attacks the problem from two directions.

"It gets us moving, naturally, which stimulates the brain stem and gives us more energy, passion, interest, and motivation. Exercise shifts our self-concept by adjusting all the chemicals including serotonin, dopamine, norepinephrine, BDNF, VEGF, and so on," explained Ratey.

When we exercise, we find that feelings of helplessness and despair begin to disappear. Working out wasn't an instant cure for me during college, but I believe it helped give me feelings of hope. My workouts provided structure and routine for my days, getting me out of my room and gave me tangible goals to work toward. It was the perfect outlet for managing my emotions.

Use Humor – World War I consisted of some of the most brutal fighting in human history. Soldiers had to endure hellish conditions at the front and more than 9 million people died. In order to cope with a world and situation they could neither predict nor understand, these soldiers relied on humor to get them through.

Canadian historian Tim Cook writes, "Humour remained an important safety valve for soldiers attempting to endure the destruction at the front." You can always laugh your stress away and take a cheerful view of adversity.

Find Community – Feeling depressed is often akin to feeling alone. Our friends and family can give us strength. Forcing us to go out and spend time with people we like can give us an emotional boost.

As Jillian Richardson, author of *Unlonely Planet*, told me, "It's important to know who you can trust with your vulnerability. Not everyone is equipped to hold someone when they're in a sensitive headspace. But if you have friends who are emotionally intelligent, lean on them. Sharing with others makes whatever you're holding feel more bearable, and less shameful. And if you don't have those friends right now, find a support group. Sometimes sharing with strangers is even more powerful, because they don't have a preexisting image of who you are. Plus, knowing that strangers share some of your problems can make you feel less alone."

Take On Challenges – Even the emperor of ancient Rome, Marcus Aurelius sometimes had trouble getting out of bed. He wrote in *Meditations*, "I am rising to do the work of a human being. Why, then, am I so irritable if I am going out to do what I was born to do and what I was brought into this world for? Or was I created for this, to lie in bed and warm myself under the bedclothes?"

Getting out of bed is often the first challenge we must face and overcome each day. Each time we tackle and complete a challenge, we become more mentally resilient.

Games provide an excellent avenue for taking on challenges. Video games give us a challenge we can defeat that is unlike anywhere else.

Games give us the opportunity to try again and again and again until we figure things out. They teach us how to approach problem solving, and give us great satisfaction when we finally overcome a challenge we have been working on.

Control Judgments – Stoic philosopher Epictetus once said, "What upsets people is not things themselves but their judgments about the things."

Remember, nothing has meaning until we give it meaning.

OVER EMOTING

Wright began playing Melee competitively in 2004, but struggled to find success. It wasn't until 2006 Wright began to gain traction with the Ice Climbers, breaking into the top 10 in a few tournaments and making a name for himself in the Melee scene.

Despite his success, Wright struggled to achieve recognition in the eyes of his opponents because he could come off as a jerk and struggled to keep his emotions in check during games.

"I expected a lot of myself in every situation. That applied to school, to other games, to social situations, you name it. I didn't just have a goal to be the best, I expected that it would happen, and every failure and error hurt tremendously," explained Wright.

Wright became known for his anger after losing matches, and it spiraled out of control in April 2016. While representing his team, Panda Global, at Smash Summit 2, Wright matched up against German Melee player "Ice." Mistake after mistake ensued for Wright. It was as if he lost control of his hands. Ice took advantage and easily defeated Wright.

Then Wright lost control.

He threw his controller out of frustration, shook his opponent's hand, and stormed off, and proceeded to punch a hole in the wall. "I thought, 'I am a disgrace,'" recounted Wright.

Wright's high expectations for himself became a major source of stress and anxiety. When he failed to meet those expectations, he lost control.

***

What happened at Smash Summit 2 is not unique to Wright.

I've experienced meltdowns in games before. I've lost my temper and played recklessly during soccer matches after a call didn't go our way. When we lose money during a Poker hand, we become liable to play foolishly. After landing on Boardwalk in Monopoly one too many times something just snaps.

The common term for this experience is *tilt*. Tilt is an emotional or mental state where we play poorly, often becoming over-aggressive because of emotional distress, frustration, mistakes, losing, and unfortunate events.

Jared Tendler, an expert in the mental game of poker explains, "When the emotional system becomes overactive, it shuts down higher brain functions." During tilt our prefrontal cortex, the area of our brain responsible for executive function, begins to shut down. This is our fight-or-flight response at work, taking us from a resting state to a high alert.

Tilt is on the far right edge of the emotional spectrum.

We often see tilt referred to in Poker or gaming. Losing a hand of Poker or a game we thought we should have won are common triggers for tilt. However, tilt can be applied anywhere. Being cut off in traffic, being constantly interrupted while working, being personally attacked during an argument, or experiencing rude customer service are everyday examples that can tilt us.

As our emotions take over we lose the ability to think clearly and get back to an emotionally neutral state (apatheia). It is like skydiving. Once we jump out of the plane (letting our emotions take over) we aren't getting back in (regaining our ability to think clearly).

Overcoming tilt is difficult, but we can regain our composure and control by following a framework developed by Lars Robl, former Danish Special Forces and sports psychologist for the Esports *Counter-Strike: Global Offensive* (CS:GO) team Astralis.

1. Acknowledge the feeling of tilt and accept it
2. Release that feeling
3. Refocusing attention and come back to the present moment

THE PATH TO EMOTIONAL CONTROL

In order to be able to acknowledge our feelings and recognize when our emotions begin to rise, we need self-awareness. If we can't name our emotions, it becomes difficult to manage them effectively.

We can improve our self-awareness through mindfulness practices, taking time to pause and reflect. Developing our self-awareness will take time and effort, but it is a foundational skill for managing emotions.

Here are some ways to practice:

Reflect Without Judgement – Anytime we experience an emotion, stop and notice it. Don't look at is as good or bad, just observe. Our internal dialogue may sound like this, "I notice I am feeling angry. That is interesting, I wonder what caused it." Pausing to reflect on our emotions without judging is good practice.

Name It – If we can give our emotions a name, it gives us the ability to respond more effectively. This could be writing it down in a journal or verbalizing it aloud to a friend.

Power Down – We are constantly "on," connected to the world through technology. Instead of immediately filling any moment of empty space with music, conversation, podcasts, games, or TV, sit in silence for a little while. We need time to just...think. Driving without the radio on or putting our phone out of sight are two easy ways to start.

Meditate – Meditation is an effective tool for gaining control of our mind. A good way to start practicing is through guided meditation. Apps like Headspace or YouTube videos are good places to find guided sessions.

The more we practice developing our self-awareness, the better we can acknowledge how we feel. Once we have acknowledged our emotions are getting out control and we are tilting, we need to accept those feelings. Emotions are a normal part of life. We may be tilted, but as an emotional feeling, it is temporary.

***

The first thing I think of when I begin to feel worked up or out of control is a quote from the movie *Seven Years in Tibet*, "If a problem can be solved there is no use worrying about it. If it can't be solved, worrying will do no good." This helps me release any pent up emotions I am feeling and prevent things from spiraling out of control.

Here are some ways we can better deal with tilt and release our feelings:

Repeat A Positive Phrase – We can use a trigger phrase to help us release emotions. For me it is the quote from *Seven Years in Tibet*. It could be "Emotions are temporary," "I know what to do," "It is time to come back to the present," or "This too shall pass." This can help us move on from that emotion.

Take A Break – Sometimes the best thing to do is to just stop, cool off, and come back later. Taking a 10-25 minute break when we feel ourselves getting heated or out of control, can stop tilt in its tracks and help us regain our composure. This is especially important after losing a few matches in a row or experiencing a string of setbacks. Use this as a cue to take a break.

Exercise – Anxiety often comes with physical sensations like rapid heartbeat, shortness of breath, and sweating. Exercise provides an opportunity to experience the symptoms of anxiety without the underlying source of fear present. "When we increase our heart rate and breathing in the context of exercise, we learn that these physical signs don't necessarily lead to an anxiety attack," explained John Ratey. We become more comfortable with these feelings and learn to recognize that they are not inherently bad.

I encourage taking breaks as the best way to regain emotional control during tilt, but we do not always have that luxury. Instead, we must prepare ourselves as best we can for the inevitable emotional rises we experience.

***

Chuck Palahniuk said, "The trick to forgetting the big picture is to look at everything close up."

Imagine you are playing in the NCAA March Madness championship game. You get fouled and go to the free throw line to take two shots. In that moment, what should you be thinking about--the result of the game or your next shot? In that moment, you control that shot, nothing more. For the best chance of making that shot, you need to give it your complete, undivided attention in the present moment.

Here are a few tactics we can use to focus our mind on the here and now:

Breathe – We seldom pay attention to our breath because it happens automatically. But there is nothing more present than our breath. Focusing on our breath forces our mind to pay attention to what is going on right now. This helps us return to a composed state.

Smile – Smiling releases feel-good neurotransmitters, dopamine and serotonin, to help us feel more relaxed. Any physical movements we make automatically are happening right now, the present.

Deliberately Focus – Our mind is constantly thinking and can easily go down a rabbit hole if we let it. To stop our mind from wandering we can deliberating focus on the task at hand. When we become totally immersed in what we need to do, right now, our mind tunes out the distractions for us.

Once we have returned to the present moment we have overcome tilt and successfully kept our emotions in check.

***

Managing our emotions isn't easy, but it pays off. "If you work on yourself, then that improvement goes everywhere with you. If you become more focused, you can focus on everything you do more. If you become better at handling your emotion, you can handle your emotion in every circumstance. It's all something you use to improve you, to go forward," explained Wright.

It doesn't matter what avenue we use to gain control of our emotions, whether it be gaming, athletics, school, or work. We can take what we learn from these areas and apply it to every area of our life.

When I feel sad or out of control, I first try to interrupt my pattern of thinking that put me in that state. The two biggest things I do when I am feeling down are to exercise and spend time with friends. I do not 'feel' like doing either of these, but I know that if I force myself to, I will begin to feel better.

When I feel frustrated and begin to rage, like when my computer keeps crashing for no reason, I find it best to separate myself from the situation until I have cooled down. I take a break and remind myself of positive phrases that help me realize that I am acting ridiculous.

I understand that emotions are part of life, but I also realize that I own my emotions. I have the power to choose how I respond and so do you.

BIOFEEDBACK

Biofeedback is an advanced technique we can use to manage our emotions. It uses electrical sensors to take in information from our body to help us control our bodily functions like heart rate.

Biofeedback helps us control normally automatic functions like our breathing, brainwaves, and heart by focusing our mind.

Neurofeedback, a form of biofeedback, uses visuals or sound to "reprogram" our brain waves. Imagine we are stuck in traffic and start to get frustrated. Our brain waves are running at a high frequency and we want to slow them down and bring us into a relaxed state. Neurofeedback can help us train our brain and learn how to slow down our brain waves and feel less stressed.

Esports players can use biofeedback to help improve their gaming performance and better manage their emotions.

"We study what creates high level performance for Esports players, what facilitates that, and how professionals can come in and reach their full potential," explained Dan Himmelstein, a performance coach and founder of Premier Esports Academy.

During biofeedback sessions, players are hooked up to sensors while playing a game like Overwatch or League of Legends. Himmelstein and his team can take the biofeedback data and overlay it with gameplay footage to generate insights into performance.

For instance, if a player started making poor decisions during a match, the team can look through the biofeedback data to find a response and then review the gameplay to identify the trigger.

"We record biofeedback data right next to the gameplay so we can tell when players are confident and in control. Their breathing is great and their heart rate variability is consistent," explained Himmelstein. These are signs that they are effectively managing their emotions.

Himmelstein and his team also use this data to find where players are struggling and determine what training is needed to help them stay in control.

Biofeedback provides valuable data that we can use to help manage our emotions.

∗∗∗

Companies are also developing new brain performance technology. HUMM Technologies created a wearable device called Edge that uses biofeedback data to improve gaming performance.

"Edge can detect when a player is tilting in real time based on their physiological responses to game events. During play, Edge monitors live biometrics such as heart rate and eye tracking to quantify a player's stress, focus, and fatigue," explained HUMM co-founder Ahumd Auleer, "In stressful and demanding situations, the software can determine when a player is beginning to tilt through this understanding of their mental and physiological state."

Esports is full of mental athletes training their brains to achieve higher levels of performance. Ian McIntyre, co-founder of HUMM, has plans to translate findings from Esports into other professions requiring high mental performance like lawyers, doctors, and fighter pilots. "We [can] take that data and combine [it] with biometric data [from Edge], and a machine learning model can effectively tell you how mental performance had an effect on the success of the activity," explained McIntyre.

HUMM is hoping that Edge can help Esports teams deal with burnout and the high level of stress players' experience. The data from Edge "can help players when they are tilting—playing poorly or frustrated—and find solutions to prevent or reduce that tilt," explained Auleer.

The Edge technology could help players train smarter by providing signs that performance is dropping off and letting them know when it is time to take a break.

KEY TAKEAWAYS

- Apatheia is state of mental composure and balance. We can use this state as a guide as we work to keep our emotions in check.
- No matter where we find ourselves on the emotional spectrum, we can control how we respond to that emotion. We can always change our emotional state.
- Overcoming depression is not easy, but there are a few things we can use to help, including- – exercise, humor, community, taking on challenges, and controlling our judgments.
- Regaining control from tilt is difficult, but not impossible. By following the steps of accepting tilt, releasing the feeling, and refocusing our attention we can regain control. Mindfulness training and taking a break are two effective strategies for overcoming tilt.

9

GAME CHANGER
DECISION MAKING

———

All we have to decide is what to do with the time that is given us.

– J.R.R. TOLKEIN

"How did you decide to run the World's Toughest Mudder?"

"One day I just decided. That's it."

We tend to overthink things and get stuck in our head. We never end up actually making a decision.

If you want to make a change in your life or do something you haven't done before, all you have to do is decide. The more you practice making decisions the better you get.

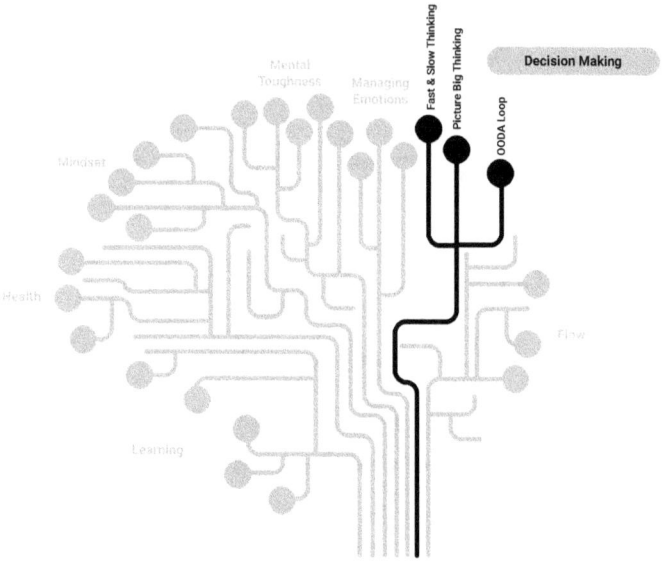

WE ARE OUR DECISIONS

At this moment, who we are is a direct reflection of the decisions we have made. "As people you are defined by the decisions that you make and the decisions that you don't make," explained Dr. Joe Arvai, a professor at the University of Calgary.

Where we live, what we eat, and whom we spend time with are all decisions that shape who we are today. If we want to change our lives, it simply comes down to making a new decision.

Decision-making is a part of life; it will never go away. The good news is that decision-making is a skill we can practice. The more we learn and practice, the better we become at making decisions.

The first step is to learn how our mind makes decisions. Once we understand how we make decisions, we can begin to change them.

MENTAL OPERATING SYSTEM

Our mind has two operating systems: fast thinking and slow thinking. In his book, *Thinking, Fast and Slow*, Daniel Kahneman refers to these as system 1 (fast) and system 2 (slow).

Our system 1 thinking is powerful, capable of processing 11 million bits of information per second and accounts for 95% of the decisions we make. "Our unconscious is really good at quick decision-making – it often delivers a better answer than more deliberate and exhaustive ways of thinking," explained Malcolm Gladwell in his book *Blink*.

Our subconscious can recognize patterns and connections before our conscious brain, even if we can't articulate why or how we know something. We call this concept thin-slicing, making quick, smart decisions, using only small bits of information.

While our unconscious mind evolved to handle massive amounts of information quickly, it can be prone to errors.

Take for instance these two examples:

A baseball and a bat cost a total of $1.10.
The bat costs $1 more than the baseball.
How much does the ball cost?

and

There is a patch of lily pads in a lake.
Each day the patch doubles in size.
If it takes 60 days for the lily pads to cover the entire lake, how long would it take to cover half the lake?

$0.10 and 30 days right? Not quite.

If we work backwards from each of these problems we find the answers are actually $0.05 and 59 days. Our fasting thinking brain wants to jump to the easiest solution. However, sometimes we need to take over control and use system 2 thinking.

Slow thinking focuses our attention on mental activities, which require conscious effort. We use this form of thinking while deciding what college to attend, working through a difficult problem, or buying a house. During deliberate decisions, the part of our brain responsible for executive function becomes more active.

We need both fast and slow thinking to make smart decisions. Understanding our mental operating system is just the beginning. It is time to start making some decisions.

THINKING SLOW

Good decision-making requires being able to take multiple perspectives. We need to think in details while being able to step back and see the big picture. Ronald Heifetz, a leadership author, calls this concept "getting off the dance floor and going on the balcony."

We need the perspective of the dance floor to understand all the pieces of a decision, while the balcony perspective helps us see how all of the pieces fit together. Decision-making requires big picture thinking. By taking multiple perspectives, we can better synthesize information and arrive at creative solutions we might have otherwise overlooked.

Big picture thinking plays an important role for Esports competitors, especially in games like League of Legends.

League of Legends is a multi-player online battle arena PC game. Two teams of five players compete to destroy the other team's Nexus (base). As in basketball, each player has a unique position and role.

On a League of Legends map, there are three lanes (top, middle, and bottom) with an area in between called the Jungle.

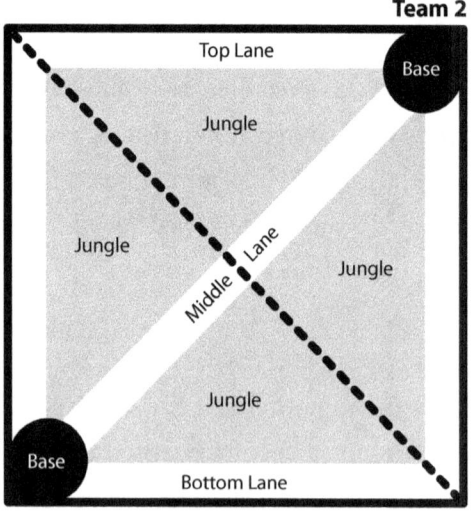

One position that requires big picture thinking is the *Jungler*.

"The Jungler needs the presence of mind to not only make decisions in the moment, but plan for decisions 90 seconds from now, and 3 minutes from now," explained Joe Bieda, a collegiate League of Legends and performance coach.

"As the game progresses a Jungler has to constantly reevaluate how the team is performing and update their planned decisions as the game progresses," added Bieda, "The longer you wait to make a decision, the worse things are going to get."

Junglers enter a match with a set of expectations about the flow of a game, but need to be aware of shifting game dynamics to be able to react appropriately. They should always be checking the map and communicating with teammates to make decisions on what to do next. Being able to take a big picture perspective and make smart decisions is a crucial skill to have.

But, is there a way to train this skill? Of course. Enter mindfulness training.

Researchers at the Wharton School found that just 15 minutes of focused-breathing meditation can lead to better decisions. Lead researcher Andrew Hafenbrack explained, "We found that a brief period of mindfulness meditation can encourage people to make more rational decisions by considering the information available in the present moment, while ignoring some of the other concerns that typically exacerbate the 'sunk cost bias.'"

Hafenbrack and his team found mediation helped to de-bias participants. "First, meditation reduced how much people focused on the past and future, and this psychological shift led to less negative emotion. The reduced negative emotion then facilitated their ability to let go of sunk costs," explained Zoe Kinias, the study's co-author.

Some professional Esports organizations, like the Immortals, are making meditation a part of their lifestyle.

Before stepping onto the stage at Overwatch tournaments, Immortal's players are quiet. Performing on stage with all of the lights, cameras, and makeup is a lot to take in. Meditation helps the players clear their minds and stay focused so they can make good decisions in game. "Meditation calms down the nerves," explained Overwatch support player Athen "Aythen" Zhu.

Immortal's Overwatch coach Zac "Chance" Palmer explained, "Mindfulness training allows [players] to first understand where they are and then make personal adjustments themselves." Mindfulness training puts the players in the driver's seat, giving them control over their mind and their decisions.

BEWARE OF BIASES

We all have biases. Biases sway our thoughts and hinder our ability to make "rational" decisions. We cannot eliminate them, but switching to slow thinking can help us avoid pitfalls. There are dozens of biases to be aware of, but here some common ones we run into.

- Anchoring – Relying too heavily on one piece of information, often the first piece we receive.
- Attention Bias – Our perception to be affected by recurring thoughts.
- Backfire Effect – When evidence dis-confirms what we believe, but instead actually strengthens our original belief.
- Bias Blind Spot – We tend to see ourselves as less biased than other people.
- Confirmation Bias – Our tendency to only look for information that supports our current point of view.
- Dunning-Kruger Effect – Unskilled people often overestimate their abilities, while experts often underestimate their abilities.
- Framing Effect – We can draw different conclusions based on how information is presented.

- Gambler's Fallacy – Thinking that future probabilities are influenced by past events when in reality, the probabilities are unchanged.
- Hindsight Bias – Seeing past events as predictable, believing we always knew.
- Illusory Correlation – Seeing a relationship between two unrelated events.
- Irrational Escalation – More commonly known as the sunk cost fallacy, putting in more investment based on prior investments even though new information shows this to be irrational. This is similar to loss aversion, coined by Daniel Kahneman, where we prefer to avoid loses than receive gains.
- Mere Exposure Effect – Liking things just because we are exposed to them often.
- Normalcy Bias – Refusing to accept the possibility of something happening that has never happened before.
- Outcome Bias – Judging decisions by outcomes rather than the quality of the decision made at the time.
- Planning Fallacy – Underestimating the time it takes to complete a task.

THINKING FAST

"Instinct is raw clay that can be shaped into a masterpiece, if you develop skills that match your talent." – Tim Grover

How are some people able to make unbelievably fast decisions?

Baseball players have to make the decision to swing or not to swing at a ball flying 100 mph in milliseconds. Professional League of Legends players make 100s of instantaneous decisions every minute. Over time, these split second decisions can make the difference between winning and losing.

Esports requires massive amounts of mental processing, taking into account everything going on in the game and rapidly processing all these pieces of information to make decisions. Amine Issa, founder of the gaming performance analytics platform Mobalytics, studied how professional League of Legends players make instinctual decisions in clutch moments.

Issa broke down the play of pro League player, Mike Yeung, during an important team fight. In the fight, Yeung pulled off a series of perfectly timed moves, all in the matter of a few seconds. With milliseconds to make each move, Yeung had to rely on gut instinct. This gut reaction is known as *game sense*.

"To an outsider, longer thinking time can seem to correlate with better decision making, but to a practiced veteran whose been in thousands of games and similar scenarios, hundreds of times, their brain is wired so that the first decision they immediately reach is usually the best one," explained Issa, "Overthinking and hesitation will usually lead to incorrect decision making."

Yeung has to rely on his unconscious brain to process these decisions. Our unconscious stores information from our experiences, so when we encounter similar scenarios in the future it is able to process them instantaneously and make smart decisions.

We can strengthen decision pathways in our brain over time thanks to myelin. Myelin is the fatty insulating sheath we learned about in chapter 2, which wraps around our nerve fibers, enabling their electrical signals to fire faster. This in essence "primes" our decision pathways to be able to react faster.

Like gamers, musicians' brains also seem to function differently. While doing complicated things with their hands, professional musicians and gamers do not activate as much of their brains as average people do.

Using fMRI, the researchers found gamers relied more on the frontal cortex, the part of our brain responsible for attention and planning, compared to non-gamers. Non-gamers have to rely more on their parietal cortex, meaning they had to spend more energy on the non-cognitive skills of hand-eye coordination. This area was more or less on autopilot for the experienced gamers.

While having our unconscious help make quick decisions is useful, we can run into problems if we are stuck in a loop of making the wrong automatic decision.

When this happens, we need to find a way to break that thought pattern and replace it with a new one.

It is like forgetting to pick up groceries after work, every single week. Our drive home becomes so automatic every day of the week we forget to take a different route past the store. We get home and realize we have no food, so we have to go back out or order something.

To stop this from happening we can consciously pre-program new decisions, so we make better automatic decisions later.

Weldon Green, a high performance Esports coach and the head coach of Counter Logic Gaming (a North American Esports team) explained that we have to put ourselves, "in a position to make the decision and then remember to make the decision." Another Esports team, TSM (Team Solo-Mid), uses position coaches to help train players to make good decisions.

One way athletes train decision making is by watching film and mentally recreating what it felt like in the moment of decision so they can pre-program their minds to make the better decision in the future. This conscious focus on future decision-making is a form of deliberate practice (chapter 4).

This may feel awkward in the beginning, but with some time and attention, we can create new automatic habits. Also, the more situations we expose ourselves to, the more naturally decisions come.

Arnold Schwarzenegger said, "You can't always win, but don't be afraid of making decisions. You can't be paralyzed by fear of failure or you will never push yourself." As we practice our decision-making skills, wrong decisions are inevitable. Making mistakes is okay.

It is best to start practicing when the stakes are low so we can refine our decision-making skills. When the stakes are low, we aren't worried as much about making the perfect decision. Practice is the best time to make bad decisions because we can stop and learn from them. This gives us the best chance to make smart decisions when the stakes are high.

HOW GAMES HELP US MAKE BETTER DECISIONS

Gamers develop skills, which make them better at *probabilistic inference*, accumulating bits of information to make decisions, enabling them to become more efficient and effective decision makers.

A 2018 study looked at the brain connectivity of real-time strategy game (RTS) Starcraft players compared to non-RTS players. The researchers found players who played Starcraft more often had a greater number of brain connections between the occipital and parietal regions. This suggests these players have better visual and spatial processing abilities.

In another study, University of Toronto psychology professor Jay Pratt found playing action video games can improve our ability to learn and take in more information. These games help us develop our *useful field of view*, a fancy way of saying how many things we can pay attention to. "Video game players are able to pick up very subtle, statistical irregularities in environments and use them to their advantage," explained Pratt.

Furthermore, games provide an environment where we get endless opportunities to practice collecting and processing information for making decisions. A 2010 study at the University of Rochester found playing video games led to faster and more accurate decision making. Action video game players developed a heightened sensitivity to the world around them, improving their decision-making capabilities.

DECISIONS UNDER PRESSURE

Even with planning and preparation, unexpected things pop up. In sports, games, and life, dynamics are constantly changing. We must learn to adapt our strategy as situations change.

Police officers and military personnel have to make life or death decisions under immense pressure. They have tools and techniques we can learn from to help us make better decisions.

One such tool is the *OODA Loop*. This is a framework created by Colonel John Boyd for making decisions in uncertain and chaotic environments.

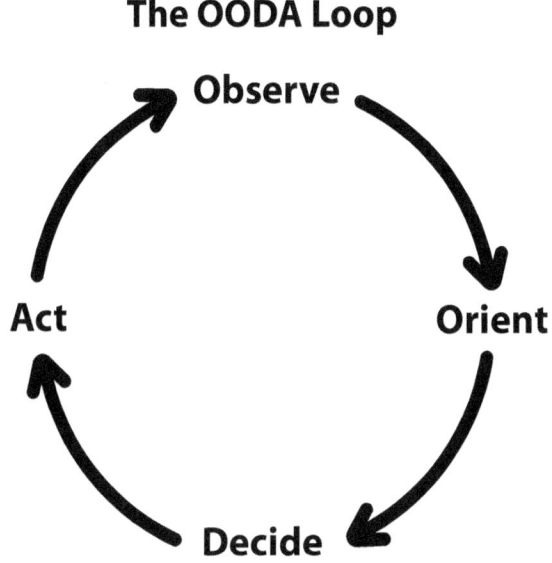

The OODA Loop

Observe

Act

Orient

Decide

The OODA Loop is broken down into four parts: observe, orient, decide, and act.

<u>Observe</u> – The first step is to observe our situation, the people around us, and the environment as a whole, including physical, emotional, and mental contexts to gain complete awareness. Poor awareness often leads to flawed decision making.

<u>Orient</u> – Orienting is about analyzing and synthesizing the information we learned during observation. This is a common area where people struggle, because they lack mental models for assessing and interpreting situations.

In this step, we call upon our previous experiences for understanding. It is easy to get stuck here without experience or proper training to be able to make sense of the information we observed. The Federal Law Enforcement Training Center explained, "The goal of training is to repeatedly expose individuals to unique situations in order for them to develop experiential learning, which will create neural shortcuts and facilitate decisive actions."

We should expose ourselves to as many new situations as possible so we can be prepared for anything. Remember the Boy Scout's motto: Be Prepared.

Decide – Now we decide. Our decision will often be implicit and instinctual.

Act – All that is left is to act.

After taking action, we move back into observation mode, assessing the impact of our action and moving through the OODA loop again. The faster we can move through the loop, the more our agility improves.

Orientation is the crucial step, which shapes our decisions. While observations are facts of reality, orientation provides the opportunity to interpret what we see and gives us the freedom to look at the world in a different way.

As we master the OODA loop, we move from process thinking to instinctual thinking. Our intuition becomes finely tuned and we can begin to move straight from observe to act.

***

There is a hierarchy of competence that follows our decision-making skill development. As we learn to make better decisions, we progress through four stages of competence, starting with unconscious incompetence and working toward unconscious competence.

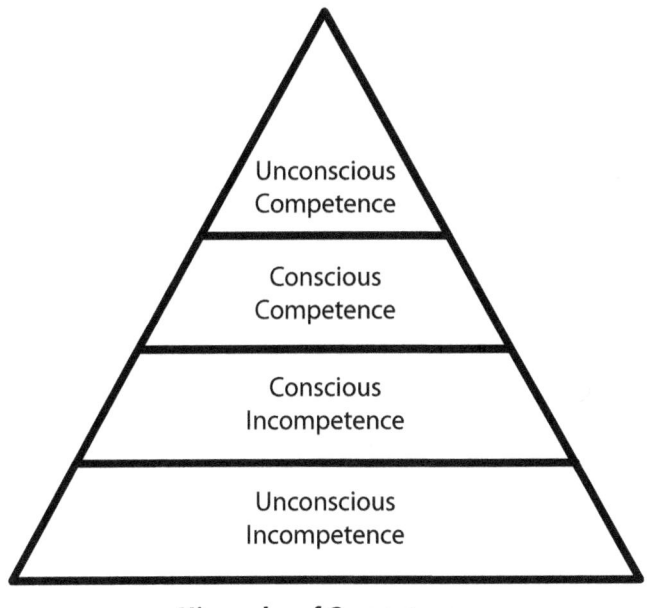

Hierarchy of Competence

For instance, when a professional golfer is getting ready to take a swing, they are not running through every single step of the swing and then deciding how to swing. They have developed an intuitive feel for the game and know exactly what to do without having to think. This is unconscious competence.

The hierarchy of competence is relevant in all areas of life. It is simply the stages of learning.

Joe Bieda uses this model to help his League of Legends players develop and progress through each stage. "The goal is to practice so much that you can get to a state of mind where you don't have to think about your decisions," explained Bieda.

Let's dive into the progression of competence through the lens of the Jungler.

Unconscious incompetence – This is the first stage of development for anyone learning something new. "When players are first starting out they have no idea what decisions are good or bad. They just don't know what they don't know," explained Bieda.

Conscious Incompetence – When players move into this stage, they know what they don't know. "Players understand their weaknesses, but not how to improve them," explained Bieda. Junglers will often make wrong decisions at this level because they still haven't mastered the fundamentals.

Players that look for what they "should" do, without understanding the "why" behind it, tend to make the wrong decisions.

In League of Legends there is a concept known as *meta*. Meta is the most effective tactic in any given situation. Many new players will look at the meta, trying learn what they should do. However, this often holds players back from improving, as they do not take the time to understand the rationale behind their decisions.

The meta is not just relevant in League of Legends as it can be applied to everyday life. For example, if you are driving to work, the highway is typically the meta path. However, if there is a traffic jam, the back roads become the meta path. "The meta changes based on the variables presented to you," explained Bieda.

Most people don't know how to navigate the back roads since they don't take the time to learn about them. The transition to conscious competence begins with the understanding of the underlying elements of the decisions you make.

Conscious Competence – Getting to this stage is a difficult leap for anyone learning something new. Reaching this level requires putting in hours of deliberate practice. "Making a mistake is the easiest way to learning something," explained Bieda, "Players should ask themselves 'What can I do to prevent that from happening next time?'"

Bieda added that new Junglers can study film on their gameplay and analyze it, learn from better players, and narrate their actions. "When you hear yourself think out loud it becomes easier to focus on what you are doing," explained Bieda.

Every time we make a mistake, we have the opportunity to learn from it and become consciously competent.

Unconscious Competence – At this stage, we have gained enough experience and credibility with ourselves that we can rely on our intuition and make good gut decisions. "Junglers at this level have an intuitive feel for where the enemy Jungler is and what they are likely doing. Experienced players develop the foresight to be able to look at a wave of enemies, understand what is going to happen, and make a decision in an instant," explained Bieda.

Once we accumulate enough experience doing things the right way, our decisions become second nature.

KEY TAKEAWAYS

- Our mind uses two primary operating systems for making decisions: slow thinking and fast thinking.

- Slow thinking is best used for big decisions that require us to see the whole picture and think through things.

- Fast thinking is best for making quick, intuitive decisions. To make quick decisions most effectively, we have to build up our skills and experience making these decisions first.

- We can use the OODA loop to progress from slow, deliberate decision making to fast, accurate decision making. The more experienced we become, the faster we can move through this loop.

- As we learn to make decisions, we move through four stages of competence. With practice and repetition, we can improve the speed of our decisions.

1 0

IN THE ZONE
FLOW

———

"If you chase two rabbits, you will lose them both."

– NATIVE AMERICAN SAYING

"Imagine you are standing in a room with 1,000 doors. You have one job; close 999 of them."

This is the essence of focus.

It is impossible to focus on one thing until we decide to ignore everything else. Deciding what not to do is a prerequisite for focus I explained.

"So, how do I decide what not to focus on?" asked my friend.

"Ask yourself, 'does this move me closer to my goals?' If not, close that door and move on."

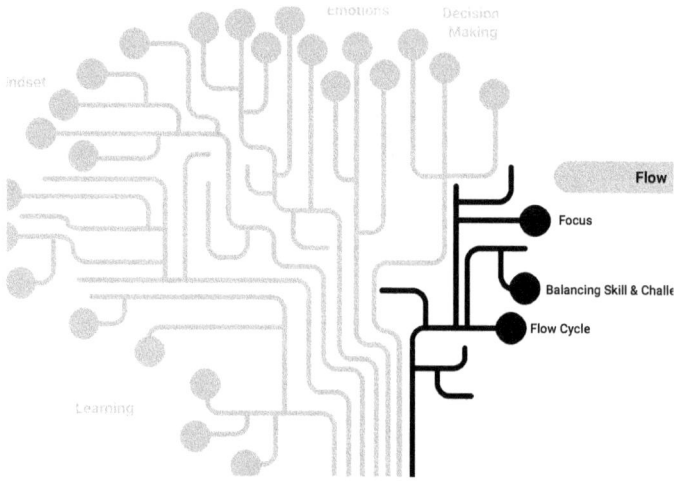

FOCUS

Clyde Beaty was born in 1903 in Bainbridge, Ohio. As a teenager, Beaty left home to join the circus and found a job cleaning cages. Over the following years he was able to move up through the ranks and become a lion tamer.

Beaty lived in an era when most lion tamers died in the ring, but he was different. He decided to try something most other lion tamers weren't doing.

He brought a chair into the ring.

But what does a chair and a lion have to do with focus? Everything.

When Beaty held the chair in front of the lion's face, it lost its ability to focus. The lion tries to focus on all four legs of the chair simultaneously, but with its attention divided, the lion becomes confused. With too many things to focus on, the lion decides to do nothing instead of attacking the person holding the chair.

We often find ourselves in the same position as the lion.

With so many things demanding our attention, we often end up trying to focus on everything. But like the lion, when we try to focus on everything, we end up focusing on nothing.

Focus requires attention. Attention is defined as "the cognitive process of selectively concentrating on one thing while ignoring other things." Where our attention goes, so does our focus.

We are capable of doing more than one thing at a time, like listening to the radio and having a conversation. However, it is impossible to completely devote our attention to multiple tasks at the same time. We are either concentrated on the music, with the conversation in the background, or vice versa.

Multitasking is actually an illusion.

Multitasking was initially a computing term used to describe one CPU alternating between tasks until completed. Since computers move so fast they appear to be truly multitasking. It is more appropriate to use the term *task switching*.

While we can split up our attention, by switching between tasks, there is a trade-off. Since we can't seamlessly transition between tasks, we pay a switching cost of efficiency and effectiveness. Each time we have to switch between tasks or a distraction pops up, we have to spend time refocusing our attention.

***

With so many things to do and options to choose from, we need to decide where to put our focus.

There are a number of ways to do this, but I believe the simpler the strategy the better when deciding where to focus. With so many options, we have to simplify.

Here is a simple strategy you can follow:

1. Write down the five most important things you have to do for the day (it is important that you stop at five)
2. Prioritize the list in order of importance
3. Concentrate only on the most important item. Work on it until completed and then move on to the next item.
4. Add new tasks to the unfinished list and repeat the process

There are other methods you can use to help focus, like *The Eisenhower Box* or the *Buffet 25-5 Rule*, however, I can't cover everything in this book.

Regardless of what strategy you use to help focus, there is one idea that makes all the difference in the world. Decide what is the most important thing you can do and do not move on to another task until you complete it. It is simple, but the results will speak for themselves.

FOCUS TOOLS

"Aristotle once said that, 'All of men's problems stem from the fact that he cannot sit in a chair, still, for hours.' In other words, we get distracted. How many of us can sit in a chair and single-mindedly work out one problem? No, after a few minutes we begin to get fidgety, we want to turn on the TV set and listen to music...when I teach physics to students, I teach them that you have to have 'butt power.' You have to have the ability to sit down, work on physics problems [un]til blood comes out of your forehead. We have no gene for physics. There's no gene for science. Science is an acquired taste... I realized every time I was struggling with all these equations, there was that pot of gold out there. I wanted to be on the cutting edge of science even if it meant that I had to not go play outside, I had to sit at my chair and simply crank out the math. You›ve got to pay your dues." – Michio Kaku, theoretical physicist.

Once we have decided where to focus our attention, we need to understand how to focus in the moment. There are three things we must practice:

- Tuning out distractions
- Concentrating
- Being present

The following tools and tactics can help us tune out distractions, concentrate, and be present:

Eliminate Distractions – The easiest way to eliminate distractions is simply to remove them. If we think back to willpower in chapter 6, putting our phone out of sight is a simple step we can take. Changing your work environment and finding a quiet place to go can quickly eliminate many potential distractions.

Water – Staying hydrated is a good way to maintain our attention. David Benton, professor of psychology at Swansea University found people who experienced greater levels of thirst performed worse on tests of attention and memory. Even with a minor loss of body weight after only an hour and a half, study participants began to show impaired attention.

Naps – Instead of reaching for another cup of coffee when we find our focus shifting, it might be a good idea to take a nap. Yes, napping is a powerful cognitive hack for productivity and attention.

Naps have been shown to double our alertness, as well as improve reaction time and logical reasoning. A 2008 experiment compared the effects of a nap, coffee, and more nighttime sleep on alertness and concentration, finding that naps were actually the most effective! It's not lazy, it's productive.

Binaural Beats – Binaural beats are special music for our brain. They are "an auditory biohack designed to facilitate brainwave entrainment," explained Aubrey Marcus, founder of Onnit. Research shows they can help improve our cognitive performance and relaxation as well.

All we need is a pair of headphones. When listening to a binaural beats track, two different frequencies are played, one in each ear. The difference of these frequencies helps to bring our brain wave frequency to the desired state. The best place to get started and find free tracks is on YouTube.

Meditation – Health expert Shaun Stevenson refers to mediation as "brain training." Meditation is a way to train our brain to be able to focus better.

MIT neuroscientist Christopher Moore conducted a study looking at the relationship between meditation and performance. Study participants were taught how to focus their attention on specific bodily sensations. After eight weeks of training, they could better control their alpha brain waves.

"These activity patterns are thought to minimize distractions, to diminish the likelihood stimuli will grab your attention. Our data indicates that meditation training makes you better at focusing, in part by allowing you to better regulate how things that arise will impact you," explained Moore.

This training works because meditation can change our brain. After eight weeks, researchers compared the meditation trained group with a control grouping, finding the trained participants showed larger changes in the size (amplitude) of their alpha brain waves when asked to focus.

Meditation also physically changes our brain, thickening regions associated with memory and sensory processing, two key factors of focus.

Flow – Flow is the ultimate form of focus. If we can tap into the flow state, we can significantly improve our focus. We will be diving into this next.

FLOW

"I tend to have these blackout moments where I don't remember actually performing the golf shot. I'd get so entrenched in the moment, my subconscious takes over," explained Tiger Woods.

We've all had moments like this: becoming totally immersed in an activity and losing all sense of time. Maybe it was playing a great video game, practicing a challenging piece of music, or competing in an important game.

This feeling is *flow*.

Psychology researcher Mihaly Csikszentmihalyi (pronounced me-hi chick-sent-me-hi) is credited with naming this concept. Csikszentmihalyi describes flow as "a state in which people are so involved in an activity that nothing else seems to matter; the experience is so enjoyable that people will continue to do it even at great cost, for the sheer sake of doing it."

This is what it feels like to be in the zone. In flow, we feel and perform at our best.

"Focus gets so intense that everything else disappears. Action and awareness start to merge. Our sense of self vanishes. Our sense of time as well. And all aspects of performance, both mental and physical, go through the roof," explained Steven Kotler, author and leading expert on human performance.

We used to think that during high performance our brain would be hyperactive. However, it turns out our brain becomes quiet. Our prefrontal cortex, the part of our brain responsible for complex thought, decision making, and for keeping track of time deactivates.

Kotler describes this state as *the deep now*.

In the deep now, we lose our sense of self. Our inner critic shuts up. Flow helps us get out of our own way.

This is partly explained by the cascade of neurochemicals produced during flow. This rush "enhances all aspects of physical performance. Muscle reaction time increases. Our sense of pain gets deadened so strength increases," explained Kotler.

We get massive cognitive benefits in 3 core areas during flow:

Motivation – Top executives at consulting firm McKinsey were 500% more productive while in flow.

Creativity – The crux of creativity is combing old ideas with new information to create something new. During flow "you take in more information per second. You pay more attention to that information. You find greater links between that information and closely related ideas, called pattern recognition. And you find greater links between that information and far-flung ideas, called lateral thinking," explained Kotler.

Learning – Flow can also accelerate our learning because the neurochemical released make it more likely that our memories will transfer from short-term to long-term storage.

The Defense Advanced Research Projects Agency (DARPA) tested this idea with military snipers. After the snipers were induced into flow, their target acquisition skills increased by 230%. Furthermore, researchers at Advanced Brain Monitoring found flow could reduce the time it took to train novice snipers into experts by 50%.

Flow is focus on steroids, drastically improving our mental performance. "Flow is the telephone booth where Clark Kent changes clothes [and] Superman emerges," said Kotler.

FINDING FLOW

Flow can be an elusive state to find. But with the right combination, we can crack the code.

Csikszentmihalyi identified 3 conditions essential for entering flow:

1. Clear Goals
2. Immediate Feedback
3. Balance of Skill and Challenge

Clear Goals – "Clear goals help [us] identify our task (so we know what to do) and align that task with belief (so we know why we're doing it)," explained Kotler. However, the most important role of clear goals is the effect it has on attention.

Cognitive scientist Daniel Simons showed his students a video of people passing around a basketball and asked them to count the passes. Once the video was complete he asked, "Did you see the gorilla?" It turns out that midway through the video a person in a gorilla costume walks into the middle of the people, beats its chest a few times, and then walk off camera. Most students did not see the gorilla.

Counting passes is a clear goal that easily sucks our attention in and lets us know where to focus. When we have a clear goal, our brain becomes narrowly focused in the present moment, blocking out all other distractions.

Immediate Feedback – Immediate feedback gives us real time information about how well we are doing so we can make changes to improve our performance. The shorter the feedback loop, the more likely we will be able to stay in the present moment.

Challenge-to-Skill Ratio – This trigger may be the most important condition for flow. The idea behind this trigger is that our attention is most engaged in the present moment when our skills are evenly balanced with challenges. The goal is to find just manageable challenges.

There are 3 distinct sections for this ratio.

1. High skill, low difficulty = boredom
2. Low skill, high difficulty = anxiety
3. Equal skill and difficulty = flow

Our goal is to take on challenges that either match up with our current skill level or are slightly greater. When our challenge is approximately equal to or slightly greater than our skills we enter the *flow channel*. Here is the Goldilocks principle in action again.

Video games are a perfect avenue for flow. Video games progressively get harder as we go along or match us up with similar skill level opponents, providing enough challenge to keep us engaged.

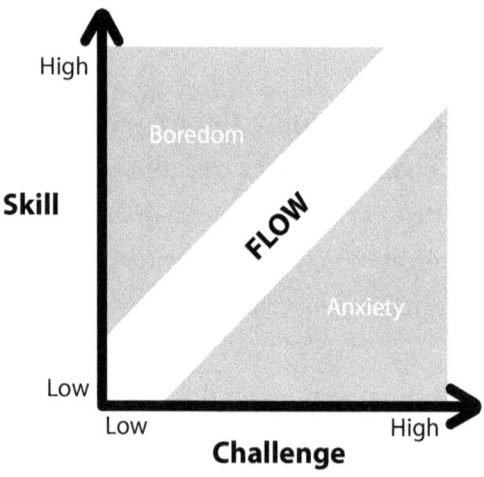

***

We can't just turn flow on or off like a light switch. Flow is a cycle with four stages. We have to move through each stage in order to reach flow.

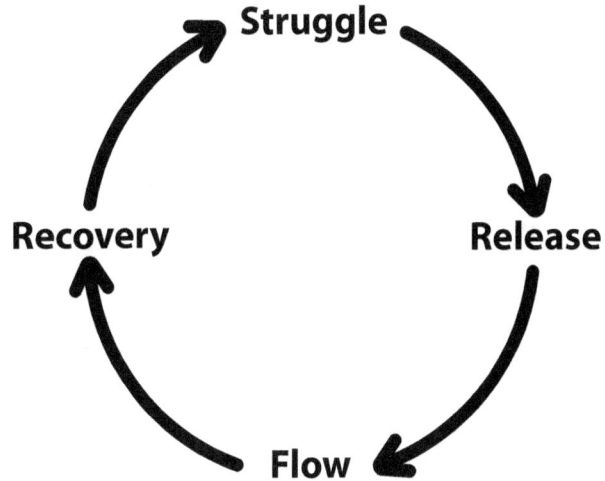

Struggle – In the first phase we are facing a challenge and overloading our mind with information. This could be engaging in demanding physical activity, analyzing complex problems, or intense studying. During this phase our stress hormones spike and increase our alertness and focus.

Release – In this phase we have to let go of our problems and take our mind off it. This could be going for a walk after studying all day. During release our brains begins to slow down, entering an alpha wave state. Our body flushes stress hormones out, making room for a flow of feel good neurochemicals. It doesn't matter how we take out mind off the struggle, all that matters is relaxation.

Flow – Once we release, we enter flow. During flow we feel calm focus amidst high stress. Neurochemicals like dopamine, serotonin, anandamide, and other endorphins release into our body. Our brain waves enter an alpha-theta zone, much like during deep meditation. In this zone we may experience bursts of high frequency brain waves called gamma waves. These waves help us bring together disparate thoughts and ideas, turning connections into creative insight.

Recovery – What comes up must come down. After flow we move into the fourth and final stage, recovery. Flow demands a lot from our body and needs time to rest and return to normal.

Flow is elusive, but with the right combination and enough practice, it can become a great tool for enhanced focus and performance.

TAKE FLIGHT

Marque Cornblatt, CEO of the Ariel Sports League, an entertainment brand and community dedicated to drone sports, has been addicted to flow since he was a child. Cornblatt grew up in a time before the X Games and Red Bull Action Series, so he had one daredevil idol to follow: Evel Knievel. He grew up doing whatever he could to create ramps and jumps for his bicycle.

Years later, Cornblatt and his friends embraced the new drone technology coming out. They wanted to build better drones for games and sports.

Thanks to technological advances enabling small, lightweight, super fast drones with a live video camera feed and headsets, which could tap into that feed, drone racing was born. Drone pilots use a remote control to fly the drones and wear a headset that allows them to see exactly what the drone sees, completely immersed.

Flying up to 70 mph, drone pilots experience the thrill of flying these machines off mountains or through obstacle courses without physical risk. "The pilot is basically in a blacked-out experience. The only sensory input they are getting is the video that's coming in and the only real movement that is required is their thumbs," explained Cornblatt.

Drone racing is an out-of-body experience, like transferring our consciousness into the drone. With this complete immersion and the challenge that comes with flying these drones, a pilot can enter a flow state.

Like flight, flow is a feeling we often long for. As Leonardo Da Vinci said, "Once you have tasted flight, you will forever walk the earth with your eyes turned skyward, for there you have been, and there you will always long to return."

KEY TAKEAWAYS

- Focus requires disciplined effort, but it is the key to achievement. The key is to direct our attention to a singular task, shutting out all other distractions.
- We can use focus tools to help us stay disciplined. Meditation and naps are good for making sure our mind feels fresh and ready to focus. Binaural beats are helpful to listen to when we need to focus as it helps shift our brainwave state.
- Flow is like a state of super focus. Finding the right challenge/skill ratio is essential for being able to enter flow. We need to take on *just manageable* challenges in order to enter flow.

11

REWIRE YOUR MIND

———

"It is easy to pretend that nobody can change anything, that society is huge and the individual is less than nothing. But the truth is individuals make the future, and they do it by imagining that things can be different."

— NEIL GAIMAN

"Training your mind is less about the end result, and more about the journey along the way," I said.

"What do you mean?"

"We need to embrace the process. We are going to make mistakes and fall down, but that is the process of how we improve," I explained.

I could tell my friend was apprehensive, so I continued. "We need to dedicate ourselves to improving our lives. What matters are the skills we acquire, the connections we make, and how much we grow."

We need to apply what we learned into our daily lives if we want to see any changes.

MAKE MISTAKES

The ceramics teacher announced on opening day that he was dividing the class into two groups. All those on the left side of the studio, he said, would be graded solely on the quantity of work they produced, all those on the right solely on its quality. His procedure was simple: on the final day of class he would bring in his bathroom scales and weigh the work of the "quantity" group: fifty pounds of pots rated an "A", forty pounds a "B", and so on. Those being graded on "quality," however, needed to produce only one pot — albeit a perfect one — to get an "A."

Well, came grading time and a curious fact emerged: the works of highest quality were all produced by the group being graded for quantity. It seems that while the "quantity" group was busily churning out piles of work – and learning from their mistakes — the "quality" group had sat theorizing about perfection, and in the end had little more to show for their efforts than grandiose theories and a pile of dead clay.

This is an excerpt from the book *Art & Fear* written by David Bayles. I think it holds a valuable lesson for us all.

It is okay to make mistakes.

Mistakes give us an opportunity to learn. The beauty of creation and getting started is that we open ourselves up to learning. An imperfect start is better than no start at all.

We won't be an expert on day one, but we can embrace the mentality of the 'quantity' art students. We have to give ourselves permission to create junk, knowing that we will get better as we go along. Trying to be perfect from day one is an easy trap to fall into.

We can apply this mentality to any skill we want to improve.

- To become a better writer, start by writing one sentence.
- To complete a marathon, start by walking one mile.
- To save for retirement, start by saving one dollar.
- To learn how to cook, start by making one recipe.
- To become a better decision maker, start by making one decision.
- To build mental toughness, start by doing one extra rep.

To begin rewiring our mind, all we have to do is take a single step in the direction of our goal. We learn something new every step of the way. To paraphrase General George S. Patton, "A good plan today is better than a perfect plan tomorrow."

CREATE CONNECTIONS

Now we need to solidify our new connections. Rewiring our brain is like building new habits.

Once our new behavior or way of thinking becomes automatic, our brain is rewired and our new connection is formed.

How long does this take? Researchers estimate that it takes on average 66 days to cement a new habit. Some of our rewiring will take longer, while other connections may come more quickly.

Rewiring Takes Time

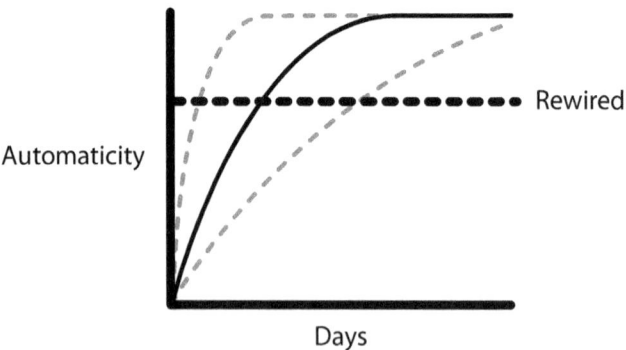

Rewiring our mind is a process, not an event. It requires changing our thoughts and behaviors. This can be challenging. However, in his book *Atomic Habits*, James Clear outlines four laws of behavior change, which can help us stick with the process of rewiring our mind.

1. **Make it Obvious** – We can set up cues to trigger our new thought pattern. If we are working on managing our emotions and we lose three games in a row, we can use that as a cue to take a break and regain control.

2. **Make it Attractive** – We need to be motivated to make a change. After losing a game, we might want to get back in and try again, but if our frustration builds then we will play worse. If we know we play better and win more often when we are calm and confident, taking time to cool off will be more attractive.

3. **Make it Easy** – If changing our behavior is difficult, we won't want to do it. Taking a break in this instance is simple and straightforward. We can pause the game or turn it off and walk away. We can set an automatic timer on our phone to go off in 20 minutes. This step is where we rewire our brain.

4. **Make it Satisfying** – When our behavior change comes with a reward, we satisfy our motivation and program our brain to remember what this feels like. After taking a break, we feel relaxed and have mental clarity. If we

don›t feel like taking a break, we can remind ourselves how we will feel after we do.

SEINFELD STRATEGY

Esports is a mental game. Professional gamers put in hours of practice to keep their minds sharp, but practicing isn't the only thing players do to train their minds.

A good way to keep track of our rewiring progress and to make it satisfying is to keep score. Keeping score provides evidence that we are taking the actions necessary to rewire our mind.

To do this we can follow the Seinfeld Strategy.

Brad Isaac was just getting his start as a young comedian when he ran across Seinfeld in a club and asked him for tips for a young comic.

He said the way to be a better comic was to create better jokes and the way to create better jokes was to write every day. But his advice was better than that. He had a gem of a leverage technique he used on himself and you can use it to motivate yourself—even when you don't feel like it.

He told me to get a big wall calendar that has a whole year on one page and hang it on a prominent wall. The next step was to get a big red magic marker.

He said for each day that I do my task of writing, I get to put a big red X over that day. "After a few days you'll have a chain. Just keep at it and the chain will grow longer every day. You'll like seeing that chain, especially when you get a few weeks under your belt. Your only job next is to not break the chain."

Our focus is about building consistency. The more we practice a new way of thinking, the stronger it becomes in our mind.

A practical way to implement this is to use a bullet journal to track habits. The premise of the calendar is the same, but we can select a few actions to complete each day and be able to visualize our progress over time.

BUILD SYSTEMS

The Greek poet Archilochus once said, "We don't rise to the level of our expectations, we fall to the level of our training."

The key to building out our skill tree and making our changes sustainable is to create systems and train properly. We need to improve our default mode of thinking because this is what we will fall back on when we run into adversity and uncertainty.

It is easy to "break the chain" when we haven't fully rewired our brain and ingrained the change in our mental operating system. When a skill or way of thinking becomes part of how we operate every day, rather than something we are working toward, it is much easier to stick with it.

As we create new connections in our brain and stick with the process, we establish a new identity.

"Each time you write a page, you are a writer. Each time you practice the violin, you are a musician. Each time you start a workout, you are an athlete," explained James Clear.

Our thoughts and behaviors are a reflection of our values and who we are. When we build and follow our systems for rewiring our brain, we change our identity. We shift our mindset from "I am trying to make decisions" to "I am a decision maker."

Consistent action reinforces our identity, as our systems are the bridge to transformational change. Rewiring our mind is a process, but with the right knowledge and tools, we all can make progress.

KEY TAKEAWAYS

- Rewiring our mind takes time, as we often have to change solid old wiring. Our brains changes just as muscles grow with use, while shrinking with neglect. We can solidify our new connections and weaken old ones through repetition.
- Rewiring our brain also changes our identity. When we forgo old ways of thinking and embrace new ones we become a new person. While this may be intimidating, it serves as the final step of rewiring.

12

HARD WIRED

———

"Our life is what our thoughts make it."

– MARCUS AURELIUS

"Now what?"

It is time to take action. The problem many of us run into is we get stuck just trying to get started. We are worried we aren't good enough yet and that we don't have the perfect path laid out.

"Crossing the finish line at World's Toughest Mudder was an incredible feeling. I had come so far and achieved what I set out for, but I also remember what it felt like to just get started."

My journey to the World's Toughest Mudder started with a single step, a single decision to start. Repetition and dedication followed.

The key to getting better at anything is to just get started, regardless of how bad we might be in the beginning. We learn by making mistakes.

Now it's your turn to rewire your brain. Don't think about it. You know what to do and how to do it. Just get started, all it takes is one step.

Rome wasn't built in a day, but it started with a single brick.

It takes time to master any skill, but we all have to start somewhere. It is easier to think about the dream of Rome, rather than put in the work to actually build it.

However, when we do think about it and realize how immense the prospect of building something is, we can quickly become overwhelmed. We can spent countless hours, days, months, and years trying to figure out the perfect plan for building our Roman empire, instead of getting started.

The simple truth is this: if we never get started, we will never have the opportunity to build something extraordinary, master a skill, or create a masterpiece. We have to trust the process and lay the first brick.

My hope is that you can take the concepts you've learned in this book and apply them to your life. Whether you want to get better at studying so you can improve your grades, master flow to become more effective at work, find ways to use your physical health to improve your mental game in Esports, or learn to control your emotions when things aren't going your way, the lessons within this book can help. The path to mastery starts at nothing and it is up to you to start building from there. It is helpful to have the end in mind, but you only have to start with a single brick.

With The Mind Skill Tree, you have a roadmap that you can use hard wire your brain and transform your mind. Each branch is interconnected, so each new skill you learn will help you master additional branches.

Training your mind starts with understanding it. Dandapani said, "Once you know how the mind works you can control it and once you can control it you can focus it. You can't focus or concentrate something you don't understand."

Training your mind is a continuous process. There is always something to work and improve. The Mind Skill Tree I have provided does not contain an exhaustive list of every mental skill out there, so I would encourage you to spend time digging into the topics that most interest you.

You now have the knowledge and tools you need to start rewiring your mind. Remember what Marcus Aurelius said, "You have power over your mind – not outside events. Realize this, and you will find strength." We are in control of our mind and the choices we make. All that's left is to decide where to begin.

APPENDIX

THANK YOU

Thank you so much for taking the time to read this book. I cover a lot in this book, so if you have any questions, would just like to chat, or are curious about book recommendations for what to read next you can reach me at the following:

Email: brandonlgustafson@gmail.com

Instagram: instagram.com/bgus22

I have a small favor to ask of you now. Would you be willing to write a short review of this book on Amazon? I read all of my reviews and love to get feedback.

Thank you again, I hope to hear from you, and best of luck training your mind!

ACKNOWLEDGEMENTS

I could not have written this book without the support of those around me. First, I must thank my girlfriend Erin, for both encouraging me to write a book in the first place and for being so supportive throughout the entire process. This book would not be the same, and may not have even been created, without her support, feedback, and guidance.

Secondly, to my friends and family, I owe an immense gratitude for the check-ins and encouragement along the way. Every little kind word was greatly appreciated.

For the content and ideas shared in this book I must give credit to those who influenced my thoughts on training our mind. This list includes, but is not limited to James Clear, Max Lugavere, Carol Dweck, Ryan Holiday, and Tom Bilyeu. If you have enjoyed this book, I would recommend checking out their work.

I would like to thank everyone on the publishing team who helped turn this idea into reality. A huge thank you to Eric Koester, Brian Bies, ChandaElaine Spurlock, Leila Summers,

Gina Champagne, Mateusz Cichosz, and Srjdan Filipovic for guiding me along the process.

I also want to thank all of my advanced readers and early interviews who helped provide feedback that shaped this book: Josef Bieda, Dave Brannan, Joel Emans, Andrew Feinstein, Kay Gustafson, Josh Hafkin, Todd Harris, Dan Himmelstein, Taylor Johnson, Rich Keller, Derek Kontny, Dylan Marvel, Logan Massman, Jake Middleton, Grant Paranjape, Cole Peyton, Emre Ruhi, and Matt Thomas.

To anyone I may have missed who impacted the creation of this book, thank you.

Lastly, I would like to thank you. Your time is valuable, and I want to thank you for spending some of it with me through this book. Thank you.

-JULY 2019

SUPPLEMENT GUIDE

BACOPA MONNIERI

- Commonly used in Ayurvedic medicine (originating in India), Bacopa monnieiri is a nootropic herb that has been shown to improve memory, improve reaction time, and improve cognitive performance by reducing anxiety. A review of additional studies found that Bacopa helped adolescents with attention, language skills, as well as memory. Bacopa is able to improve areas of cognition by promoting neuron communication. It helps nerve endings, called dendrites, grow, which facilitates communication and improves memory performance. Bacopa also boosts antioxidants in your brain, can inhibit the formation of Beta-amyloid plaques, and improve blood flow to your brain.

- Examine.com recommendation: 300mg (55% bacoside content). There are some "instant" effects from bacopa, helping reduce anxiety and stress during challenging cognitive tests, although optimal benefits are seen after 8-12 weeks of supplementation. Best when consumed with a meal or other fat sources for improved absorption.

CAFFEINE AND L-THEANINE

- Caffeine, commonly found in coffee, helps you feel alert. Your almost habitual morning buzz. L-theanine, commonly found in green tea, helps you feel relaxed and calm. Together they are the yin and the yang of focus--alertness and concentration without an extreme rush or devastating crash. You can think of L-theanine as "taking the edge off" stimulants. Green tea is a good source for caffeine and L-theanine. For an added bonus, add some lemon juice to your tea. Researchers at Purdue found that adding citrus juice to tea, like a lemon, improves the bio-availability of the green tea catechins and antioxidants.

- Examine.com recommendation: 200 mg/200 mg combination of caffeine and L-theanine (1:1 ratio).

CHOLINE

- Choline is used in building and maintaining your cell membranes. CDP-Choline (citicoline) is a nootropic compound and precursor to both choline and uridine and research shows benefits primarily in focus and memory, while also helping to reduce swelling and blood-brain barrier breakdown after brain injury.

- Examine.com recommendation: Either 500-2000 mg CDP-choline or 300-1200 mg of Alpha GPC taken in divided doses during the day. More is not necessarily better. Research suggests that attention performance is better at the lower dose for CDP-choline and other studies have shown similar effects with Alpha-GPC.

CREATINE

- Creatine plays a role in energy production by helping make ATP and it has neuroprotective effects. Creatine is most commonly used in fitness circles as a way to help build and maintain muscle and it is one the most researched and safest molecules out there. It also can benefit your brain, improving cognitive processing and performance. A review of creatine trials found that supplementing also improved reasoning and short-term memory in healthy individuals.

- NIH recommendation: 3-5 g of creatine monohydrate. Creatine provides optimal benefits when taken over time. There is no need to load creatine (take large amounts when first beginning supplementation).

GINKGO BILOBA

- Ginkgo biloba (EGb-761) is one of the most widely used herbs for brain health. It works by improving oxygen flow to your brain, benefiting aspects like attention and memory.
- Examine.com recommendation: 120-240 mg (24% glycosides) prior to performance. Goes well with phosphatidylserine for memory performance and speed of memory. Best when consumed with a meal.

PHOSPHATIDYLSERINE

- Phosphatidlyserine (PS) is a fat-soluble phospholipid commonly found in your brain since your body produces it. It is part of your protective cellular membrane, keeping it flexible and helping to get rid of waste. Supplementing with additional PS has been shown to improve memory, reduce stress, and boost cognition.
- Examine.com recommendation: 300 mg (100 mg taken 3 times daily). 200-400 mg doses also show benefits to

attention in adolescents and adults. Best when consumed with a meal or other fat sources for improved absorption.

RHODIOLA ROSEA

- Rhodiola rosea is an herb and adaptogen, which has been used for reducing fatigue and exhaustion during periods of stress. If you are dealing with extended periods of stress, including repetitive work, and avoiding the burnout effect, rhodiola may be a good option to try.
- Examine.com recommendation: 50-680 mg of rhodiola rosea (either SHR-5 extract or extract containing 3% rosavins and 1% salidrosides). There is no need to supplement beyond 680 mg as higher does may be ineffective. Some people experience stimulatory effects so if this impacts your sleep, try to avoid taking late at night.

TURMERIC

- A signature spice in Indian food, turmeric is an antioxidant and used to fight off inflammation. The primary active ingredient in turmeric is called curcumin, which helps protect your brain against cognitive decline by keeping your neurons healthy. Curcumin has been shown to improve memory and concentration by increasing blood blow.
- Examine.com recommendation: 500 mg curcumin and 20 mg piperine (3 times daily). Curcumin is often consumed

with piperine (black pepper extract) to improve bioavailability. Best when consumed with food.

URIDINE

- Uridine has been shown to improve neuron growth produced by BDNF, improve memory function, and protect your brain from oxidative stress. It has also been shown to help your brain repair more quickly and effectively.
- Examine.com recommendation: 500-1000 mg of uridine monophosphate. Uridine monophosphate goes well with choline and DHA.

VITAMIN B6, B9, & B12

- B vitamins can reduce stress and support neurotransmitter production. Poultry, fish, eggs, potatoes, nutritional years, vegetables, and fruit are all foods that contain one or more of these B vitamins.
- NIH recommendation: For most adults 1.3 mg of vitamin B6, 400 mcg of vitamin B9 and 2.4 mcg of vitamin B12.

VITAMIN D

- Vitamin D can reduce brain fog and depression by ensuring your body can synthesize serotonin. Many adults are estimated to have below optimal levels of vitamin D. Try getting more early-morning sun exposure to increase vitamin D levels before supplementing.

- Examine.com recommendation: 1000-2000 IU of vitamin D3 (*cholecalciferol*). Best when consumed with a meal or other fat sources for improved absorption.

VITAMIN K

- Vitamin K is fat soluble with two varieties: K1 and K2. K1 supports blood coagulation, while K2 is more active, supporting overall cognitive function, stronger bones, memory and insulin regulation. Optimal levels of vitamin K helps calcium stay in the areas you want it, like bones and teeth.
- NIH recommendation: 90-120 mcg of vitamin K2 (*menaquinone-7 or MK-7*). Pairs well with vitamin D. Best when consumed with a meal or other fat sources for improved absorption.

ADDERALL

Commonly prescribed to help people with ADHD focus, Adderall is probably not this panacea of the ultimate levels of human focus that you might think it is.

Oftentimes, Adderall is not the right choice, and it can even work against you. In 2013, a Psychopharmacology study found that Adderall actually impaired performance in healthy adults who already had above average levels of cognitive function. Another study in 2013 looking at the cognitive effectiveness of Adderall in healthy people found, "Despite the lack of enhancement observed...participants nevertheless believed their performance was more enhanced by the active capsule than by placebo." Unless you have been prescribed Adderall by your doctor or medical professional, it may do more harm than good when it comes to actual cognitive enhancement.

WORKOUT

Workout for Improving Brain Function

-By Jake Middleton, Founder of Esports Trainer, LLC (Esportstrainer.gg)

Start with a 5-minute warm-up of jogging in place to increase body temperature and blood flow to muscles.

1. Body Weight Push Up – 3 sets of 10 reps
2. Body Weight Squat with Calf Raise – 3 sets of 15 reps
3. Elbow Plank – 3 sets of 20-30 seconds
4. Jumping Jacks – 3 sets of 30 seconds

Modifying Difficulty – Each of these exercises is modifiable based on your fitness level. If you are unable to do pushups or the elbow plank, you can lower the difficulty by moving from your feet to your knees. For the body weight squat, you can eliminate the calf raise and/or add a chair underneath you when squatting.

Rest Periods – Keep your heart rate up and increase blood flow by reducing rest periods keeping them around 30 seconds. You could also do a circuit and move from one exercise to the next with no rest – 10 pushups, 15 squats, and 20-30 second elbow plank, repeat 2 more times for total of 3 sets.

MEDITATION

Beginners Meditation

-By Andrew Feinstein, Author of *Find Your Mind*

Start by finding a position that is nice and comfortable. It helps if you sit up straight, relax your shoulders, and plant your feet on the floor.

If this is your first time meditating, it might be useful to find a nice, quiet and comfortable space, but if you happen to be sitting on a subway car reading this, do not be dissuaded from giving it a try.

Obviously, reading a meditation is very different from listening to one. I can't really tell you to close your eyes right now because how would you read on? But, I can give you some structure, some tips and then I can send you on your way to embrace the silence on your own.

I know this seems a little strange and most of you will want to just keep reading on, but I highly recommend that when I tell you to, you put this book down and just take 1-5 minutes to just sit in silence and practice what I lay out below.

So before we do anything, let's just take three nice deep breaths in.

Breathing in through your nose and out through your mouth.

As you breathe in, really try to fill your lungs with air – it is said that on a daily basis we only use 25% of our lungs capacity, meaning we take short and choppy breaths so here is your opportunity to take some nice deep ones.

As you breathe out, let go of all of the stress and tension in your body – let your shoulders sink away from your ears and let your chest and abdomen release. We hold so much tension in our bodies and now is the perfect opportunity to let it out.

Today, we are going to do a breath focus meditation-meaning that we are going to make our breath the object of our focus. So when you go off into your own silence, you will be tasked with anchoring your attention to your breath and every time you notice you are distracted, you will simply return to the breathing.

Pretty simple, right?

Well, simple doesn't mean easy.

So to get you started, take one more breath in through your nose. If you pay attention to this breath, you will notice that you can feel it in four key areas.

Top of the lip / Tip of the nose – you will notice a cooling sensation when you breathe in, and a warming sensation when you breath out

Throat – you might notice a slight tingling /cooling as the air passes through

Chest – you will notice that your chest expands on an inhale and contracts on an exhale

Stomach – you will notice that your stomach inflates and deflates like a balloon

So in your short practice, see if you can focus on one of these sensations. If you can just feel the air enter and leave your body through one of these points. The analogy I often give is picturing yourself as an outside observer, watching your breathing as if you were watching the flow of a river stream.

This is all that you need to do for the next few minutes. But, remember, that if you get distracted, don't get angry, don't beat yourself up. It doesn't mean that you are bad at meditation, you are just not experienced, yet. So every time you realized you are distracted, gently remind yourself to return to the breathing and with this practice, you will, over time, build your ability to focus your attention where you want it.

So to recap, try to watch your breathing, and every time you get distracted, try to return once again to the object at hand, your breath.

Now take a few moments and enjoy the silence.

NOTES

Here is detailed list of all the references I used in each chapter of the book. This should be sufficient for most readers, but I do understand that scientific literature changes over time and realize that some citations may need to be updated with time. I also am fully aware that I likely made a mistake somewhere in this book, either improperly attributing information or not providing credit where appropriate. If you do believe there is a mistake, please contact me at brandonlgustafson@gmail. com so I fix the issue. Thank you!

CHAPTER 1

28   **"Our culture has become hooked on the quick-fix"**: Goggins, David. *Can't Hurt Me*. Lioncrest Publishing, 2018.
29   **Goggins signed up for a 24 hour race:** 1. Think, Big. "Strengthen Your Mind Like a Navy SEAL | David Gog-

gins." YouTube, YouTube, 2 Nov. 2017, www.youtube.com/watch?v=vyJ_hhninDw.

31 **"the views you adopt for yourself"**: "Chapter 1: The Mindsets." Mindset, by Carol S. Dweck, Robinson, 2017, p. 6.

32 **"The passion for stretching yourself"**: "Chapter 1: The Mindsets." Mindset, by Carol S. Dweck, Robinson, 2017, p. 7.

32 **"If we gave students a growth mindset"**: Trudeau, Michelle. "Students' View of Intelligence Can Help Grades." NPR, NPR, 15 Feb. 2007, www.npr.org/templates/story/story.php?storyId=7406521.

33 **At the end of the semester:** Trudeau, Michelle. "Students' View of Intelligence Can Help Grades." NPR, NPR, 15 Feb. 2007, www.npr.org/templates/story/story.php?storyId=7406521.

33 **"He who says he can"**: Sagar. "He Who Says He Can and He Who Says He Can't Are Both Usually Right. – Confucius." Sagar Basak, 25 May 2017, sagarbasak.com/he-who-says-he-can-and-he-who-says-he-cant-are-both-usually-right-confucius.

34 **Bradley Cooper in Limitless:** Burger, Neil, director. Limitless. 2011.

CHAPTER 2

42 **Reptilian brain:** "The Evolutionary Layers Of The Human Brain." *The Brain From Top To Bottom*, thebrain.mcgill.ca/flash/d/d_05/d_05_cr/d_05_cr_her/d_05_cr_her.html.

43 **billions of brain cells:** Herculano-Houzel, Suzana. "The human brain in numbers: a linearly scaled-up primate brain." Frontiers in human neuroscience 3 (2009): 31.

43 **Our brain uses about 20%:** Raichle, Marcus E., and Debra A. Gusnard. "Appraising the brain's energy budget." Proceedings of the National Academy of Sciences 99.16 (2002): 10237-10239.

43 **Our brain uses about 20%:** Cody, Ervin, et al. "How to Increase Blood Flow to the Brain." Be Brain Fit, 9 Jan. 2019, bebrainfit.com/increase-blood-flow-brain/.

43   **Poor blood flow can cause effects:** "Circulatory System Problems - Symptoms of Poor Circulation." NativeRemedies, www.nativeremedies.com/ailment/poor-blood-circulation-symptoms.html.

43   **Poor blood flow can cause effects:** Laskowski, M.D. Edward R. "Sitting Risks: How Harmful Is Too Much Sitting?" Mayo Clinic, Mayo Foundation for Medical Education and Research, 8 May 2018, www.mayoclinic.org/healthy-lifestyle/adult-health/expert-answers/sitting/faq-20058005

43   **ensure our brain is getting good blood flow:** Wendel, Lizzie. "21 Natural Ways to Improve Blood Circulation." HealthyLine™, 8 Apr. 2019, healthyline.com/20-natural-ways-to-improve-blood-circulation/.

44   **Each type of wave has its own characteristics:** "Meet Your Brain Waves - Introducing Alpha, Beta, Theta, Delta, And Gamma." FinerMinds, FinerMinds, 23 Jan. 2017, www.finerminds.com/mind-power/brain-waves/.

45   **gateway to the subconscious mind:** "Chapter 16: Calm Your Inner Chatter." Sleep Smarter: 21 Essential Strategies to Sleep Your Way to a Better Body, Better Health, and Bigger Success, by Shawn Stevenson, Rodale Books, 2016, pp. 138–140.

46   **Our body begins to relax:** "The Biology of Sleep." Healthy Eating Tips to Prevent, Control, and Reverse Diabetes, 4 Dec. 2018, www.helpguide.org/harvard/biology-of-sleep-circadian-rhythms-sleep-stages.htm.

47   **called neurotransmitters:** "The Synapse." Khan Academy, Khan Academy, www.khanacademy.org/science/biology/human-biology/neuron-nervous-system/a/the-synapse

48   **involved in attention, motivation, movement, and perception:** Björklund, Anders, and Stephen B. Dunnett. "Dopamine neuron systems in the brain: an update." Trends in neurosciences 30.5 (2007): 194-202.

48   **every time we "discover" something:** Weinschenk Ph.D., Susan. "The Dopamine Seeking-Reward Loop." Psychology Today, Sussex Publishers, 28 Feb. 2018, www.psychologytoday.com/us/blog/brain-wise/201802/the-dopamine-seeking-reward-loop.

48   **dopamine itself keeps us awake:** "Chapter 5: Depression."
      Spark: the Revolutionary New Science of Exercise and the
      Brain, by John J. Ratey and Eric Hagerman, Little, Brown,
      2013, pp. 121.

48   **promotes relaxation and positive social interactions:**
      Young, Simon N., and Marco Leyton. "The role of serotonin
      in human mood and social interaction: insight from altered
      tryptophan levels." Pharmacology Biochemistry and Behav-
      ior71.4 (2002): 857-865.

49   **regulating our body's internal clock:** staff, Science X. "Neu-
      rotransmitter Serotonin Shown to Link Sleep–Wake Cycles
      with the Body's Natural 24-Hour Cycle." Medical Xpress
      - Medical Research Advances and Health News, Medical
      Xpress, 22 Feb. 2013, medicalxpress.com/news/2013-02-neu-
      rotransmitter-serotonin-shown-link-sleepwake.html

49   **called out** second brain: Hadhazy, Adam. "Think Twice: How
      the Gut's 'Second Brain' Influences Mood and Well-Being."
      Scientific American, 12 Feb. 2010, www.scientificamerican.
      com/article/gut-second-brain/.

49   **increase our serotonin levels:** Young, Simon N. "How to
      increase serotonin in the human brain without drugs." Jour-
      nal of psychiatry & neuroscience: JPN 32.6 (2007): 394.

49   **important for managing anxiety:** Rogers, Kara. "Norepi-
      nephrine." Encyclopædia Britannica, Encyclopædia Bri-
      tannica, Inc., 26 Apr. 2018, www.britannica.com/science/
      norepinephrine.

49   **Our body has both excitatory and inhibitory:** "What Is
      Glutamate? An Examination of the Functions, Pathways and
      Excitation of the Glutamate Neurotransmitter." Neurohacker
      Collective, neurohacker.com/what-is-glutamate.

49   **important both remain balanced:** Yizhar, Ofer, et al.
      "Neocortical Excitation/Inhibition Balance in Information
      Processing and Social Dysfunction." Nature News, Nature
      Publishing Group, 27 July 2011, www.nature.com/articles/
      nature10360?page%5Cu003d25.

49   **exercise may help replenish these:** "This Is Your Brain on
      Exercise." ScienceDaily, ScienceDaily, 25 Feb. 2016, www.
      sciencedaily.com/releases/2016/02/160225101241.htm.

50   **protects our neurons:** "Chapter 2: Learning." *Spark: the Revolutionary New Science of Exercise and the Brain,* by John J. Ratey and Eric Hagerman, Little, Brown, 2013, pp. 40.

50   **Strength training and various forms of aerobic exercise:** Alban, Deane. "How to Increase BDNF, Key Protein for Healthy Brain Cells." Be Brain Fit, 24 Apr. 2019, bebrainfit. com/increase-bdnf/.

50   **We can mold and shape:** "What Is Neuroplasticity? Definition + 14 Brain Plasticity Exercises." Positive Psychology Program - Your One-Stop PP Resource!, 4 Sept. 2018, positivepsychologyprogram.com/neuroplasticity/.

50   **We can mold and shape:** Sentis. "Neuroplasticity." YouTube, YouTube, 6 Nov. 2012, www.youtube.com/watch?v=ELpfY-CZa87g.

52   **neurons that fire together:** Gerstner, Wulfram. "Hebbian learning and plasticity." From neuron to cognition via computational neuroscience (2011): 0-25.

52   **Through repeated activity:** Alberts, Bruce. "How Cells Obtain Energy from Food." Current Neurology and Neuroscience Reports., U.S. National Library of Medicine, 1 Jan. 1970, www.ncbi.nlm.nih.gov/books/NBK26882/.

52   **Through repeated activity:** "Chapter 2: Learning." *Spark: the Revolutionary New Science of Exercise and the Brain,* by John J. Ratey and Eric Hagerman, Little, Brown, 2013, pp. 39-40.

52   **process called myelination:** Kirkwood, Caitlin. "Myelin: An Overview." BrainFacts.org, BrainFacts, 24 Mar. 2015, www. brainfacts.org/Brain-Anatomy-and-Function/Anatomy/2015/ Myelin

52   **"With the repetition, you're creating":** "Chapter 2: Learning." *Spark: the Revolutionary New Science of Exercise and the Brain,* by John J. Ratey and Eric Hagerman, Little, Brown, 2013, pp. 56.

53   **"Information is transferred subconsciously":** Labs, eAthlete. "HOW ARE ESPORTS PLAYERS SO FAST? The Brain Science of Pro Gaming." YouTube, YouTube, 15 Dec. 2018, www.youtube.com/watch?v=NZyy9bKyEyg.

53 **boosts information processing and reaction speed:** Labs, eAthlete. "HOW ARE ESPORTS PLAYERS SO FAST? The Brain Science of Pro Gaming." YouTube, YouTube, 15 Dec. 2018, www.youtube.com/watch?v=NZyy9bKyEyg.

53 **It simply requires:** Sentis. "Neuroplasticity." YouTube, YouTube, 6 Nov. 2012, www.youtube.com/watch?v=ELpfY-CZa87g.

CHAPTER 3

58 **"Stress is a threat":** "Chapter 3: Stress." Spark: the Revolutionary New Science of Exercise and the Brain, by John J. Ratey and Eric Hagerman, Little, Brown, 2013, pp. 59.

59 **silent killer:** Gallup, Inc. "Eight in 10 Americans Afflicted by Stress." Gallup.com, 20 Dec. 2017, news.gallup.com/poll/224336/eight-americans-afflicted-stress.aspx.

60 **"As iron sharpens iron":** "Proverbs 27:17 NIV." Read the Bible. A Free Bible on Your Phone, Tablet, and Computer. | The Bible App | Bible.com, www.bible.com/bible/111/PRO.27.17.NIV.

61 **"You get stronger/faster/healthier/more resistant":** Sisson, Mark. "Hormesis: How Certain Kinds of Stress Can Actually Be Good for You." Mark's Daily Apple, 8 Nov. 2012, www.marksdailyapple.com/hormesis-how-certain-kinds-of-stress-can-actually-be-good-for-you/.

61 **Waitzkin was walking:** "Bio." Josh Waitzkin, www.joshwaitzkin.com/josh.

62 **"Growth comes at the point of resistance":** Waitzkin, Josh. The Art of Learning: a Journey in the Pursuit of Excellence. Free Spirit, 2008.

63 **Once we internalize this knowledge:** "Rethinking Stress." Peak Performance: Elevate Your Game, Avoid Burnout, and Thrive With the New Science of Success, by Steve Magness and Brad Stulberg, St Martins Pr, 2017, pp. 44–46.

65 **indicator of systemic recovery:** Cook, Christian J., and Blair T. Crewther. "The social environment during a post-match video presentation affects the hormonal responses and play-

ing performance in professional male athletes." Physiology & behavior 130 (2014): 170-175.

66 **Performance Arousal Curve:** Yerkes, Robert M., and John D. Dodson. "The Relation of Strength of Stimulus to Rapidity of Habit-Formation." The Canadian Journal of Chemical Engineering, Wiley-Blackwell, 7 Oct. 2004, onlinelibrary. wiley.com/doi/abs/10.1002/cne.920180503.

69 **zero wins in 110 years:** "Tour De France 2017: Is Chris Froome Britain's Least Loved Great Sportsman? - BBC Sport." BBC News, BBC, www.bbc.com/sport/cycling/40692045.

69 **"The whole principle came from":** "Olympics Cycling: Marginal Gains Underpin Team GB Dominance - BBC Sport." BBC News, BBC, www.bbc.com/sport/olympics/19174302.

70 **even go to the hotel:** Harrell, Eben. "How 1% Performance Improvements Led to Olympic Gold." Harvard Business Review, 30 Oct. 2015, hbr.org/2015/10/how-1-performance-improvements-led-to-olympic-gold.

70 **8 more gold medals:** Myers, Joe. "This Coach Improved Everything by 1%. This Is the Remarkable Difference It's Made." World Economic Forum, www.weforum.org/agenda/2016/08/this-coach-improved-everything-by-1-this-is-the-remarkable-difference-it-s-made/.

70 **including 7 world records:** "World and Olympic Records Set at the 2012 Summer Olympics." Wikipedia, Wikimedia Foundation, 10 Nov. 2018, en.wikipedia.org/wiki/World_and_Olympic_records_set_at_the_2012_Summer_Olympics#Cycling.

70 In 2012 Bradley Wiggins: 13. Longmore, Andrew. "Bradley Wiggins." Encyclopedia Britannica, Encyclopedia Britannica, Inc., 14 Sept. 2018, www.britannica.com/biography/Bradley-Wiggins.

70 **Chris Froome, won the Tour de France:** Sparks, Karen. "Chris Froome." Encyclopedia Britannica, Encyclopedia Britannica, Inc., 21 June 2018, www.britannica.com/biography/Chris-Froome.

71 **"The Power of Tiny Gains":** James Clear. "Marginal Gains: This Coach Improved Every Tiny Thing by 1 Percent." James Clear, 13 Nov. 2018, jamesclear.com/marginal-gains.

CHAPTER 4

79 **became an Expert Generalist:** Simmons, Michael. "How Elon Musk Learns Faster and Better than Everyone Else." Quartz, Quartz, 31 July 2018, qz.com/968101/how-elon-musk-learns-faster-and-better-than-everyone-else/.

79 **"Someone who has the ability and curiosity":** Simmons, Michael. "How One Life Hack From A Self-Made Billionaire Leads To Exceptional Success." Forbes, Forbes Magazine, 28 Aug. 2015, www.forbes.com/sites/michael-simmons/2015/03/23/how-one-life-hack-from-a-self-made-billionaire-leads-to-exceptional-success/#1f94fb38543d.

80 **read two books a day:** Vance, Ashlee. "Elon Musk, the 21st Century Industrialist." Bloomberg.com, Bloomberg, 14 Sept. 2012, www.bloomberg.com/news/articles/2012-09-13/elon-musk-the-21st-century-industrialist#p2.

80 **Transfer is the ability to extend:** "Read 'How People Learn: Brain, Mind, Experience, and School: Expanded Edition' at NAP.edu." National Academies Press: OpenBook, www.nap.edu/read/9853/chapter/6.

80 **"You can't learn without memorizing":** "Chapter 9: The Talented Tenth." Moonwalking with Einstein: a Journey through Memory and the Mind, by Joshua Foer, Allen Lane, 2011, pp. 195–195.

81 **"It is important to view knowledge":** "r/IAmA - I Am Elon Musk, CEO/CTO of a Rocket Company, AMA!" Reddit, www.reddit.com/r/IAmA/comments/2rgsan/i_am_elon_musk_ceocto_of_a_rocket_company_ama/.

82 **develop the skills of learning:** Chi, Michelene T.H., et al. "Self-Explanations: How Students Study and Use Examples in Learning to Solve Problems." The Canadian Journal of Chemical Engineering, Wiley-Blackwell, 11 Feb. 2010, onlinelibrary.wiley.com/doi/abs/10.1207/s15516709cog1302_1.

82 **build connections and draw parallels between:** Gentner, Dedre, et al. "Learning and Transfer: A General Role for Analogical Encoding." Journal of Personality and Social Psychology, American Psychological Association Inc., 20 Mar. 2016, www.scholars.northwestern.edu/en/publications/learning-and-transfer-a-general-role-for-analogical-encoding.

82 **FAST learning model:** Mindvalley. "Speed Learning: Learn In Half The Time | Jim Kwik." YouTube, YouTube, 7 Dec. 2017, www.youtube.com/watch?v=or1LTe5KkSA.

83 **exposed to more than 5,000 ads:** Story, Louise. "Anywhere the Eye Can See, It's Likely to See an Ad." The New York Times, The New York Times, 15 Jan. 2007, www.nytimes. com/2007/01/15/business/media/15everywhere.html.

83 **"Information + Emotion":** Mindvalley. "Speed Learning: Learn In Half The Time | Jim Kwik." YouTube, YouTube, 7 Dec. 2017, www.youtube.com/watch?v=or1LTe5KkSA.

84 **"While we teach, we learn":** "Seneca Quotes." BrainyQuote, Xplore, www.brainyquote.com/quotes/seneca_405315.

84 **It takes on average 10,000 hours:** Gladwell, Malcolm. Outliers: The Story of Success. Back Bay Books, Little, Brown and Company, 2008.

84 **10,000 hours of deliberate practice:** Ericsson, K. Anders, Ralf T. Krampe, and Clemens Tesch-Römer. "The role of deliberate practice in the acquisition of expert performance." Psychological review 100.3 (1993): 363.

84 **intentional and systematic approach:** Ericsson, Anders, et al. "The Making of an Expert." Harvard Business Review, 1 Aug. 2014, hbr.org/2007/07/the-making-of-an-expert.

85 **"vast amounts of knowledge":** "Chapter 3: The Expert Expert." Moonwalking with Einstein: a Journey through Memory and the Mind, by Joshua Foer, Allen Lane, 2011, pp. 63–66.

85 **parietal cortices were especially active:** Amidzic, Ognjen, Hartmut J. Riehle, and Thomas Elbert. "Toward a psychophysiology of expertise: Focal magnetic gamma bursts as a signature of memory chunks and the aptitude of chess players." Journal of Psychophysiology 20.4 (2006): 253-258.

86 **we hit the OK plateau:** Behance, Inc. "Joshua Foer: Step Outside Your Comfort Zone and Study Yourself Failing." 99U By Behance, 9 Mar. 2016, 99u.adobe.com/videos/7061/ Joshua-Foer-Step-Outside-Your-Comfort-Zone-and-Study-Yourself-Failing.

86 **Ericcson found experts have:** Ericsson, K. Anders. "The influence of experience and deliberate practice on the devel-

opment of superior expert performance." The Cambridge handbook of expertise and expert performance 38 (2006): 685-705.

86   **Ericcson found experts have:** "Chapter 8: The OK Plateau." Moonwalking with Einstein: a Journey through Memory and the Mind, by Joshua Foer, Allen Lane, 2011, pp. 171.

87   **blocking seems intuitive:** Pan, Steven C. "The Interleaving Effect: Mixing It Up Boosts Learning." Scientific American, 4 Aug. 2015, www.scientificamerican.com/article/the-interleaving-effect-mixing-it-up-boosts-learning/.

88   **interleaving consists of practicing each area:** "The Learning to Learn Series." Academic Affairs, academicaffairs.arizona.edu/Interleaving.

88   **We have traditionally followed a massed learning:** Talks, TEDx. "Spiraling the Curriculum to Get Sticky Learning | Kristin Phillips | TEDxKitchenerED." YouTube, YouTube, 16 June 2016, www.youtube.com/watch?v=4jLANkgniSM.

89   **when we interleave topics our brain:** Talks, TEDx. "Spiraling the Curriculum to Get Sticky Learning | Kristin Phillips | TEDxKitchenerED." YouTube, YouTube, 16 June 2016, www.youtube.com/watch?v=4jLANkgniSM.

89   **when we interleave topics our brain:** Dunlosky, John, et al. "Improving students' learning with effective learning techniques: Promising directions from cognitive and educational psychology." Psychological Science in the Public Interest 14.1 (2013): 4-58.

89   **since 1885:** Ebbinghaus, Hermann. "Memory: A contribution to experimental psychology." Annals of neurosciences20.4 (2013): 155.

90   **the average score:** Pan, Steven C. "The Interleaving Effect: Mixing It Up Boosts Learning." Scientific American, 4 Aug. 2015, www.scientificamerican.com/article/the-interleaving-effect-mixing-it-up-boosts-learning/.

90   **the average score:** Rohrer, Doug, Robert F. Dedrick, and Kaleena Burgess. "The benefit of interleaved mathematics practice is not limited to superficially similar kinds of problems." Psychonomic bulletin & review 21.5 (2014): 1323-1330.

91   **When we alternate topics during practice:** Rohrer, Doug. "Interleaving helps students distinguish among similar concepts." Educational Psychology Review 24.3 (2012): 355-367.

92   **There once was a Greek poet:** "Cicero, De Oratore Book 2." de_or_1, pages.pomona.edu/~cmc24747/sources/cic_web/de_or_2.htm.

94   **using MRI technology she found:** Maguire, E A et al. "Navigation-related structural change in the hippocampi of taxi drivers" Proceedings of the National Academy of Sciences of the United States of America vol. 97,8 (2000): 4398-403.

94   **winning the World Memory Championship:** "Mullen Memory." Mullen Memory, mullenmemory.com/.

95   **Mullen uses the same technique:** Ghosal, Gourav. "The Hound of Baskervilles Mind Palace." YouTube, YouTube, 16 July 2016, www.youtube.com/watch?v=0FSKTndbwVo.

95   **The memory palace helps us take:** "Chapter 5: The Memory Palace." Moonwalking with Einstein: a Journey through Memory and the Mind, by Joshua Foer, Allen Lane, 2011, pp. 91.

96   **We are going to place mental images:** "Chapter 5: The Memory Palace." Moonwalking with Einstein: a Journey through Memory and the Mind, by Joshua Foer, Allen Lane, 2011, pp. 91.

96   **The crazier the things we see:** "Chapter 5: The Memory Palace." Moonwalking with Einstein: a Journey through Memory and the Mind, by Joshua Foer, Allen Lane, 2011, pp. 100.

CHAPTER 5

101   **In 2011, Cavin Balaster fell 20 feet:** "Preface" How to Feed a Brain: Nutrition for Optimal Brain Function and Repair, by Cavin Balaster, Feed A Brain LLC, 2017, p. 1-3.

101   **Balaster developed a nutritional plan:** "Chapter 3: The Ins and Outs Overview" How to Feed a Brain: Nutrition for Optimal Brain Function and Repair, by Cavin Balaster, Feed A Brain LLC, 2017, p. 29.

102 **system of neurons that stretches across:** Furness, John B., and Marecello Costa. "Types of nerves in the enteric nervous system." Commentaries in the Neurosciences. 1980. 235-252.

102 **We find about 95% of our serotonin:** Mart, M. T., F. Azpiroz, and J. R. Malagelada. "Melatonin and the gastrointestinal tract." Therapie 53.5 (1998): 453-458.

103 **They helps us digest food, absorb nutrients:** Hair, Marilyn, and Jon Sharpe. "Fast Facts About The Human Microbiome." The Center for Ecogenetics and Environmental Health, 2014, depts.washington.edu/ceeh/downloads/FF_Microbiome.pdf.

103 **Our gut is a direct connection to our brain:** UnderwoodSep, Emily, et al. "Your Gut Is Directly Connected to Your Brain, by a Newly Discovered Neuron Circuit." Science, 26 Sept. 2018, www.sciencemag.org/news/2018/09/your-gut-directly-connected-your-brain-newly-discovered-neuron-circuit.

105 **Our body is 60% water:** Perlman, Howard, and Usgs. "The Water in You." Adhesion and Cohesion Water Properties, USGS Water Science School, water.usgs.gov/edu/propertyyou.html(http://water.usgs.gov/edu/propertyyou.html).

105 **we can only survive 4-7 days without water:** Spector, Dina. "Here's How Long a Person Can Survive without Water." The Independent, Independent Digital News and Media, 26 Mar. 2018, www.independent.co.uk/life-style/health-and-families/health-news/how-long-a-person-can-survive-without-water-a6873341.html.

105 **performance on attention related tasks declines:** "Dehydration: Two Hours Affects Body, Brain." Healthline, Healthline Media, www.healthline.com/health-news/2-hours-dehydration-can-affect-body-and-brain#4.

105 **our brains can shrink when it becomes:** Biller, A., et al. "Responses of the human brain to mild dehydration and rehydration explored in vivo by 1H-MR imaging and spectroscopy." American Journal of Neuroradiology (2015).

105 **Decreasing our water intake by just 3-4%:** Popkin, Barry M., Kristen E. D'Anci, and Irwin H. Rosenberg. "Water, hydration, and health." Nutrition reviews 68.8 (2010): 439-458.

105 **Even a 1-2% drop in body weight:** Ganio, Matthew S., et al. "Mild dehydration impairs cognitive performance and mood of men." British Journal of Nutrition106.10 (2011): 1535-1543.

105 **Even a 1-2% drop in body weight:** Armstrong, Lawrence E., et al. "Mild Dehydration Affects Mood in Healthy Young Women, 2." The Journal of nutrition 142.2 (2011): 382-388.

105 **Even a 1-2% drop in body weight:** Gopinathan, P. M., G. Pichan, and V. M. Sharma. "Role of dehydration in heat stress-induced variations in mental performance." Archives of Environmental Health: An International Journal 43.1 (1988): 15-17.

106 **these vegetables are a staple for our brain health:** Xavier, Ana Augusta Odorissi, and Antonio Pérez-Gálvez. "Carotenoids as a Source of Antioxidants in the Diet." Carotenoids in Nature. Springer, Cham, 2016. 359-375.

106 **A 2017 study found that consuming leafy greens:** Morris, Martha Clare, et al. "Nutrients and bioactives in green leafy vegetables and cognitive decline: Prospective study." Neurology 90.3 (2018): e214-e222.

106 **Sea vegetables are particularly rich in iodine:** Knudsen, Nils, et al. "Comparative study of thyroid function and types of thyroid dysfunction in two areas in Denmark with slightly different iodine status." European Journal of Endocrinology 143.4 (2000): 485-491.

106 **good for muscle growth and can protect us:** Doyle, Marek. "Marek Doyle." Blueprint Fitness |Nutritionist and Hormonal Specialist, 11 Dec. 2009, www.blueprintfitness.co.uk/iodine-the-forgotten-nutrient/.

107 **alternating between kelp and dulse supplements:** "Chapter 10: The Ins - Superfoods." How to Feed a Brain: Nutrition for Optimal Brain Function and Repair, by Cavin Balaster, Feed A Brain LLC, 2017, p. 92-93.

107 **sulforaphane is a genetic modulator that helps activate:** Frank, Kurtis. "The Complete Guide to Sulforaphane (And 10 Foods High in Sulforaphane)." Legion Athletics, Legion Athletics, 15 Aug. 2018, legionathletics.com/sulforaphane/.

107 **support the health of our blood vessels:** Wang, Rui. "Physiological implications of hydrogen sulfide: a whiff exploration that blossomed." Physiological reviews 92.2 (2012): 791-896.

107 **support the health of our blood vessels:** Cipolla, Marilyn J. "The cerebral circulation." Integrated systems physiology: From molecule to function1.1 (2009): 1-59.

107 **helps circulate nutrients throughout our body:** Dolan, Raymond J., et al. "Regional cerebral blood flow abnormalities in depressed patients with cognitive impairment." _Journal of Neurology, Neurosurgery & Psychiatry_55.9 (1992): 768-773.

108 **scavenging oxidants, lowering blood pressure:** Borek, Carmia. "Garlic reduces dementia and heart-disease risk." The Journal of nutrition 136.3 (2006): 810S-812S.

108 **reduce the length of our colds:** Josling, Peter. "Preventing the common cold with a garlic supplement: a double-blind, placebo-controlled survey." Advances in therapy 18.4 (2001): 189-193.

109 **between 250-1000 mg per day:** Examine.com. "Fish Oil: Proven Health Benefits, Dosage, and More." Examine.com, Examine.com, 9 May 2019, examine.com/supplements/fish-oil/.

109 **boost cognition, improve memory, and even:** Reger, Mark A., et al. "Effects of β-hydroxybutyrate on cognition in memory-impaired adults." _Neurobiology of aging_25.3 (2004): 311-314.

109 **boost cognition, improve memory, and even:** Rebello, Candida J., et al. "Pilot feasibility and safety study examining the effect of medium chain triglyceride supplementation in subjects with mild cognitive impairment: a randomized controlled trial." BBA clinical 3 (2015): 123-125.

109 **MCT oil enhances the effects of DHA and EPA:** Kondreddy, Vijay Kumar Reddy, Maheswaraiah Anikisetty, and Kamatham Akhilender Naidu. "Medium-chain triglycerides and monounsaturated fatty acids potentiate the beneficial effects of fish oil on selected cardiovascular risk factors in rats." The Journal of nutritional biochemistry 28 (2016): 91-102.

110 **Fructose can impair its own absorption:** Lugavere, Max, et al. "The Sour Truth About Sweet Fruit." Experience Life, 20 Mar. 2018, experiencelife.com/article/genius-foods/.

110 **The darker the pigment of fruit:** Hayman, Vicki. "Nutrition Rainbow Of Pigment Power." Nutrition and Food Safety, 19 Oct. 2018, uwyoextension.org/uwnutrition/2017/10/05/nutrition-rainbow-of-pigment-power/.

110 **boost mood and improve memory function:** Krikorian, Robert, et al. "Blueberry supplementation improves memory in older adults." Journal of agricultural and food chemistry 58.7 (2010): 3996-4000.

110 **boost mood and improve memory function:** Williams, Claire M., et al. "Blueberry-induced changes in spatial working memory correlate with changes in hippocampal CREB phosphorylation and brain-derived neurotrophic factor (BDNF) levels." Free Radical Biology and Medicine 45.3 (2008): 295-305

110 **twice the amount of Vitamin C as oranges:** Nippard, Jeff. "KIWI FRUIT: THE ONE TRUE SUPERFOOD | Kiwi Nutritional Science Explained." YouTube, YouTube, 9 Sept. 2017, www.youtube.com/watch?v=bMD1he9CMWg.

111 **protect our brain:** Martínez-Lapiscina, Elena H., et al. "Mediterranean diet improves cognition: the PREDIMED-NA-VARRA randomised trial." J Neurol Neurosurg Psychiatry (2013): jnnp-2012.

111 **supporting enzymes that break down:** Abuznait, Alaa H., et al. "Olive-oil-derived oleocanthal enhances β-amyloid clearance as a potential neuroprotective mechanism against Alzheimer's disease: in vitro and in vivo studies." ACS chemical neuroscience 4.6 (2013): 973-982.

111 **improve blood flow to our brain:** Brickman, Adam M., et al. "Enhancing dentate gyrus function with dietary flavanols improves cognition in older adults." Nature neuroscience 17.12 (2014): 1798.

111 **A longitudinal study published in 2016 found:** Crichton, Georgina E., Merrill F. Elias, and Ala'A. Alkerwi. "Chocolate intake is associated with better cognitive function: The Maine-Syracuse Longitudinal Study." Appetite 100 (2016): 126-132.

111 **Clinical trials showed that cocoa drinks:** Mastroiacovo, Daniela, et al. "Cocoa flavanol consumption improves cognitive function, blood pressure control, and metabolic profile in elderly subjects: the Cocoa, Cognition, and Aging (CoCoA) Study—a randomized controlled trial–." The American journal of clinical nutrition101.3 (2014): 538-548.

111 **Max Lugavere, author of** Genius Foods, **recommends:** "Genius Food #4: Dark Chocolate." Genius Foods: Become Smarter, Happier, and More Productive, While Protecting Your Brain Health for Life, by Max Lugavere, HarperCollins Publishers, 2018, pp. 115–116.

112 **A study performed by the University of Maryland:** Zagursky, Erin. "It's Not All in Your Head - It's in Your Gut, Too." William and Mary, 9 June 2015, www.wm.edu/news/stories/2015/fermented-food-social-anxiety-study123.php.

112 **Avoid fermented foods on the shelf:** Parvez, S., et al. "Probiotics and their fermented food products are beneficial for health." _Journal of applied microbiology_100.6 (2006): 1171-1185.

113 **grass-fed beef contains nutrients and minerals:** "Genius Food #6: Grass-Fed Beef." Genius Foods: Become Smarter, Happier, and More Productive, While Protecting Your Brain Health for Life, by Max Lugavere, HarperCollins Publishers, 2018, pp. 173.

113 **give our brain a boost in serotonin:** Yamadera, Wataru, et al. "Glycine ingestion improves subjective sleep quality in human volunteers, correlating with polysomnographic changes." _Sleep and Biological Rhythms_5.2 (2007): 126-131.

113 **organ meats are also full of nutrients:** Williams, Peter. "Nutritional composition of red meat." Nutrition & Dietetics 64 (2007): S113-S119.

113 **"Good broth will resurrect the dead":** "Bone Broth and Its Bountiful Benefits." Return2Health, 5 Sept. 2016, www.return2health.net/articles/bone-broth-bountiful-benefits/.

115 **"Sleep is the single most effective thing":** Walker, Matthew P. Why We Sleep: Unlocking the Power of Sleep and Dreams. Scribner, an Imprint of Simon & Schuster, Inc., 2018.

116 **helps regulate attention during the day:** Sansone, Randy A., and Lori A. Sansone. "Sunshine, serotonin, and skin: a partial explanation for seasonal patterns in psychopathology?." Innovations in clinical neuroscience10.7-8 (2013): 20.

116 **follows the rising and setting of the sun:** Duffy, Jeanne F., and Charles A. Czeisler. "Effect of light on human circadian physiology." Sleep medicine clinics 4.2 (2009): 165-177.

116   **serotonin is converted into melatonin:** "Biological Rhythms - How It Works." Science Clarified, www.scienceclarified. com/everyday/Real-Life-Biology-Vol-3-Earth-Science-Vol-1/ Biological-Rhythms-How-it-works.html.

116   **light exposure at night prevents melatonin production:** Harvard Health Publishing. "Blue Light Has a Dark Side." Harvard Health Blog, Harvard Health Publishing, www. health.harvard.edu/staying-healthy/blue-light-has-a-dark-side.

117   **Our brain consolidates information:** "Sleep, Learning, and Memory." Benefits of Sleep | Healthy Sleep, healthysleep. med.harvard.edu/healthy/matters/benefits-of-sleep/learning-memory.

117   **the glymphatic system comes out at night:** Iliff, Jeff. "One More Reason to Get a Good Night's Sleep." Ted, Ted, 2014, www.ted.com/talks/jeff_iliff_one_more_reason_to_get_a_ good_night_s_sleep?language=en.

117   **the glymphatic system comes out at night:** "To Sleep, Perchance to Clean." Ice Packs vs. Warm Compresses For Pain - Health Encyclopedia - University of Rochester Medical Center, 17 Oct. 2013, www.urmc.rochester.edu/news/story/3956/ to-sleep-perchance-to-clean.aspx.

118   **After 24 hours of sleep deprivation:** Heffernan, Margaret. "Too Little Sleep: The New Performance Killer." CBS News, CBS Interactive, 9 Feb. 2011, www.cbsnews.com/news/too-little-sleep-the-new-performance-killer/.

118   **After 24 hours of sleep deprivation:** Heffernan, Margaret. Willful Blindness: Why We Ignore the Obvious at Our Peril. Walker, 2012.

118   **parietal lobe and prefrontal cortex lose between:** Heffernan, Margaret. "Too Little Sleep: The New Performance Killer." CBS News, CBS Interactive, 9 Feb. 2011, www.cbsnews.com/ news/too-little-sleep-the-new-performance-killer/.

118   **A study published in the American Academy:** "Poor Sleep Equal to Binge Drinking, Marijuana Use in Predicting Bad Grades." American Academy of Sleep Medicine – Association for Sleep Clinicians and Researchers, 7 Nov. 2017, aasm. org/poor-sleep-equal-to-binge-drinking-marijuana-use-in-predicting-academic-problems/.

118 **"We now know that 24 hours without sleep":** Czeisler, C
A. "Sleep Deficit: the Performance Killer. A Conversation
with Harvard Medical School Professor Charles A. Czeisler." Current Neurology and Neuroscience Reports., U.S.
National Library of Medicine, Oct. 2006, www.ncbi.nlm.
nih.gov/pubmed/17040040.

119 **As of 2013:** Gallup, Inc. "In U.S., 40% Get Less Than Recommended Amount of Sleep." Gallup.com, 19 Dec. 2013, news.
gallup.com/poll/166553/less-recommended-amount-sleep.
aspx.

119 **light negatively impacted body temperatures:** "Chapter
5 - Section: Sleeping, Dreaming, & Dying." Lights out: Sleep,
Sugar, and Survival, by T. S. Wiley and Bent Formby, Atria
Paperback, 2014.

120 **Caffeine has a half life of 6 hours:** Purdy, Kevin. "What Caffeine Actually Does to Your Brain." Lifehacker, Lifehacker.
com, 24 June 2013, lifehacker.com/5585217/what-caffeine-ac-
tually-does-to-your-brain.

120 **reduce sleep time by an hour:** Paddock PhD, Catharine.
"Caffeine Can Disrupt Sleep Hours Later." Medical News
Today, MediLexicon International, 15 Nov. 2013, www.med-
icalnewstoday.com/articles/268851.php.

120 **Blue light from our devices can leave you:** "How Technology
Impacts Sleep Quality." Sleep.Org, Sleep.Org, www.sleep.org/
articles/ways-technology-affects-sleep/.

121 **"Around 10:00 p.m., your body goes through":** "How Technology Impacts Sleep Quality." Sleep.Org, Sleep.Org, www.
sleep.org/articles/ways-technology-affects-sleep/.

121 **body secretes higher doses of melatonin:** "Lux." Wikipedia, Wikimedia Foundation, 18 Dec. 2018, en.wikipedia.org/
wiki/Lux."How Technology Impacts Sleep Quality." Sleep.
Org, Sleep.Org, www.sleep.org/articles/ways-technology-af-
fects-sleep/.

121 **"If your body is chronically deprived of the regenerative
sleep":** "Chapter 5 - Section: Sleeping, Dreaming, & Dying."
Lights out: Sleep, Sugar, and Survival, by T. S. Wiley and
Bent Formby, Atria Paperback, 2014.

121   **"Keeping computers, TVs, and work materials"**: "Twelve Simple Tips to Improve Your Sleep." Twelve Simple Tips to Improve Your Sleep | Healthy Sleep, 2007, healthysleep.med. harvard.edu/healthy/getting/overcoming/tips.

122   **"Exercise is the single most powerful tool"**: "Chapter 10: The Regimen." Spark: the Revolutionary New Science of Exercise and the Brain, by John J. Ratey and Eric Hagerman, Little, Brown, 2013, pp. 245–245.

122   **improves brain function by supporting the growth**: "Introduction." Spark: the Revolutionary New Science of Exercise and the Brain, by John J. Ratey and Eric Hagerman, Little, Brown, 2013, pp. 5–5.

122   **"First, it optimizes your mind-set"**: "Chapter 2: Learning." Spark: the Revolutionary New Science of Exercise and the Brain, by John J. Ratey and Eric Hagerman, Little, Brown, 2013, pp. 53-53.

123   **Hebbian plasticity**: "Hebbian Theory." Wikipedia, Wikimedia Foundation, 27 May 2019, en.wikipedia.org/wiki/ Hebbian_theory.

123   **"When we exercise, particularly"**: "Chapter 2: Learning." Spark: the Revolutionary New Science of Exercise and the Brain, by John J. Ratey and Eric Hagerman, Little, Brown, 2013, pp. 41-41.

123   **"In a 2007 study, German researchers"**: "Chapter 2: Learning." Spark: the Revolutionary New Science of Exercise and the Brain, by John J. Ratey and Eric Hagerman, Little, Brown, 2013, pp. 45-45.

123   **Complex activities and aerobic exercise**: Bergland, Christopher. "Once and for All: Aerobic Exercise Increases Brain Size." Psychology Today, Sussex Publishers, 14 Nov. 2017, www.psychologytoday.com/us/blog/the-athletes-way/201711/ once-and-all-aerobic-exercise-increases-brain-size.

123   **"While aerobic exercise elevates neurotransmitters"**: "Chapter 2: Learning." Spark: the Revolutionary New Science of Exercise and the Brain, by John J. Ratey and Eric Hagerman, Little, Brown, 2013, pp. 55-55.

124   **"With the repetition, you're also creating thicker myelin"**: "Chapter 2: Learning." Spark: the Revolutionary New Science

of Exercise and the Brain, by John J. Ratey and Eric Hagerman, Little, Brown, 2013, pp. 56-56.

125 **MRI scans showed higher levels of brain activity:** Hillman, C H et al. "The effect of acute treadmill walking on cognitive control and academic achievement in preadolescent children" Neuroscience vol. 159,3 (2009): 1044-54.

126 **"Beyond just training":** Tsuji, Alysha. "How Rick Fox Is Changing the Culture, Strategy of ESports -- at Least at One Team." USA Today, Gannett Satellite Information Network, 15 Oct. 2017, ftw.usatoday.com/2017/10/rick-fox-esports-echo-fox-brandini-changing-culture-fitness-workout-stigma-video-games-real-sport.

128 **"We were particularly impressed by both":** Schütz, Martin. "Science Shows That ESports Professionals Are Real Athletes | DW | 12.03.2016." DW.COM, 2016, www.dw.com/en/science-shows-that-esports-professionals-are-real-athletes/a-19084993.

CHAPTER 6

132 **"There are these two young fish swimming":** "This Is Water by David Foster Wallace (Full Transcript and Audio)." Farnam Street, 18 May 2018, fs.blog/2012/04/david-foster-wallace-this-is-water/.

133 **On May 6, 1854, Roger Bannister:** Taylor, Bill. "What Breaking the 4-Minute Mile Taught Us About the Limits of Conventional Thinking." Harvard Business Review, 10 Apr. 2018, hbr.org/2018/03/what-breaking-the-4-minute-mile-taught-us-about-the-limits-of-conventional-thinking.

133 **"For years milers had been striving":** Bryant, John. 3:59.4: The Quest to Break the 4 Minute Mile. Hutchinson, 2004.

134 **more than 1,400 runners, including high schoolers:** "World Sub-4 Mile Alphabetic Register." USATF Championships Attendance Trends, trackandfieldnews.com/stats-and-more/statistics/world-sub-4-mile-alphabetic-register/.

135 **we can choose to believe different:** Mindvalley. "Super Entrepreneur Tom Bilyeu On How Your Belief Becomes

Truth." YouTube, YouTube, 24 Feb. 2017, www.youtube.com/
watch?v=nL57gNIpqoU.

137   **"Ghrelin levels dropped about three times":** Crum, Alia
J., et al. "Mind over milkshakes: mindsets, not just nutrients, determine ghrelin response." _Health Psychology_30.4
(2011): 424.

137   **"Ghrelin levels dropped about three times":** Spiegel, Alix.
"Mind Over Milkshake: How Your Thoughts Fool Your Stomach." NPR, NPR, 14 Apr. 2014, http://www.npr.org/sections/
health-shots/2014/04/14/299179468/mind-over-milkshake-
how-your-thoughts-fool-your-stomach(http://www.npr.org/
sections/health-shots/2014/04/14/299179468/mind-over-
milkshake-how-your-thoughts-fool-your-stomach).

140   **"the ability or belief to believe in yourself":** Talks, TEDx.
"The Skill of Self Confidence | Dr. Ivan Joseph | TEDxRyer-
sonU." YouTube, YouTube, 13 Jan. 2012, www.youtube.com/
watch?v=w-HYZv6HzAs&list=PL400F4prLMhiP1wzj8X-
HtdfExvlBCjVoN&index=5.

142   **"A confident and positive mindset can be both":** Clear,
James. "World Chess Champion Garry Kasparov on How
to Build Confidence." James Clear, 12 June 2018, jamesclear.
com/kasparov-confidence.

143   **"Top grandmasters flinch under the tension of his style":**
Waitzkin, Fred. "King Kasparov." The New York Times, The
New York Times, 7 Oct. 1990, www.nytimes.com/1990/10/07/
magazine/king-kasparov.html.

143   **"Mr. Kasparov had lost confidence":** Greenhouse, Steven. "With a Draw, Kasparov Keeps Title." The New York
Times, The New York Times, 27 Dec. 1990, www.nytimes.
com/1990/12/27/nyregion/with-a-draw-kasparov-keeps-title.
html.

143   **"Kasparov was an intimidator over the board":** Waitzkin,
Josh. The Art of Learning: a Journey in the Pursuit of Excellence. Free Spirit, 2008.

144   **retained his title of World Chess Champion:** "World Chess
Championship 1990." Wikipedia, Wikimedia Foundation, 16
Nov. 2018, en.wikipedia.org/wiki/World_Chess_Champion-
ship_1990.

146 **becoming the first ever drone racing champion**: "What It Takes to Be a Drone Racer." Engadget, www.engadget.com/2017/10/19/jordan-temkin-drone-racing-team-big-whoop/.

146 **"I know from my previous background"**: "What It Takes to Be a Drone Racer." Engadget, www.engadget.com/2017/10/19/jordan-temkin-drone-racing-team-big-whoop/.

147 **secured his second DRL championship**: "What It Takes to Be a Drone Racer." Engadget, www.engadget.com/2017/10/19/jordan-temkin-drone-racing-team-big-whoop/.

148 **brain is not good at differentiating between**: Schacter, Daniel L., et al. "The future of memory: remembering, imagining, and the brain." Neuron 76.4 (2012): 677-694.

149 **our mind will think it is a real memory**: Pelletier, Emilie. "4 Scientific Reasons Why Visualization Will Increase Your Chances to Succeed." MAQTOOB For Entrepreneurs, MAQTOOB For Entrepreneurs, 24 Jan. 2018, entrepreneurs.maqtoob.com/4-scientific-reasons-why-visualization-will-increase-your-chances-to-succeed-5515ef2dbdb7.

149 **"The objective is to create such a lifelike experience"**: Ferriss, Tim. "The Tim Ferriss Show Transcripts: Michael Gervais." The Blog of Author Tim Ferriss, 7 June 2018, tim.blog/2018/05/30/the-tim-ferriss-show-transcripts-michael-gervais/.

150 **"We think about self-esteem in one of two ways"**: Bilyeu, Tom. "Why Self-Esteem Is the Secret to Success." YouTube, YouTube, 27 June 2018, www.youtube.com/watch?v=WvUKfdXGmGQ.

150 **"When your ego is that attached"**: Bilyeu, Tom. "Why Self-Esteem Is the Secret to Success." YouTube, YouTube, 27 June 2018, www.youtube.com/watch?v=WvUKfdXGmGQ.

150 **"If I pride myself on being smart"**: Bilyeu, Tom. "Why Self-Esteem Is the Secret to Success." YouTube, YouTube, 27 June 2018, www.youtube.com/watch?v=WvUKfdXGmGQ.

151 **"I am the master of my fate"**: Henley, William Ernest. "Celebrating English Poets & Poetry." Poets.org, Academy

of American Poets, 18 Sept. 2018, www.poets.org/poetsorg/
poem/invictus.

152 **"Self-compassion is not about a judgement"**: "How To
Be More Confident: 3 Secrets Backed By Research." Bark-
ing Up The Wrong Tree, 10 Apr. 2016, www.bakadesuyo.
com/2016/04/how-to-be-more-confident-2/.

153 **"The experts in** The Brain **documentary"**: "How the Navy
Seals Increased Passing Rates." Psychology Today, Sussex
Publishers, www.psychologytoday.com/us/blog/communica-
tion-central/200911/how-the-navy-seals-increased-passing-
rates.

155 **older group of meditators outperformed:** van Leeuwen,
Sara, Notger G. Müller, and Lucia Melloni. "Age effects on
attentional blink performance in meditation." Consciousness and Cognition 18.3 (2009): 593-599.

156 **meditation could help you prevent the breakdown:** Lazar,
Sara W., et al. "Meditation experience is associated with
increased cortical thickness." Neuroreport 16.17 (2005): 1893.

156 **the fight-or-flight part of your brain, shrunk:** Hölzel, Britta
K., et al. «Mindfulness practice leads to increases in regional
brain gray matter density.» Psychiatry Research: Neuroim-
aging 191.1 (2011): 36-43.

CHAPTER 7

161 **"when ships were made of wood":** Schultz, Colin. "Shackleton Probably Never Took Out an Ad Seeking Men for a Hazardous Journey." Smithsonian.com, Smithsonian Institution,
10 Sept. 2013, www.smithsonianmag.com/smart-news/shack-
leton-probably-never-took-out-an-ad-seeking-men-for-a-
hazardous-journey-5552379/.

162 **"I called to the other men that the sky":** "Ernest Shackleton Quotes." BrainyQuote, Xplore, www.brainyquote.com/
authors/ernest_shackleton.

162 **"Difficulties are just things to overcome":** "Ernest Shackleton Quotes." BrainyQuote, Xplore, www.brainyquote.com/
authors/ernest_shackleton.

163 **"Super-human effort isn't worth a damn"**: "Ernest Shackleton Quotes." BrainyQuote, Xplore, www.brainyquote.com/authors/ernest_shackleton.

163 **Shakelton's story is one of adventure:** "Ernest Shackleton." Biography.com, A&E Networks Television, 25 Jan. 2019, www.biography.com/people/ernest-shackleton-9480091.

163 **Shakelton's story is one of adventure:** Creative, National Geographic. "Survival! The Shackleton Story." YouTube, YouTube, 10 May 2014, www.youtube.com/watch?v=sgh_77TtX5I.

163 **"The impediment to actions advances action"**: Posted by Daily Stoic on May 4, 2018. "The Obstacle Is The Way by Ryan Holiday: Book Summary, Key Lessons and Best Quotes." Daily Stoic Stoic Wisdom For Everyday Life History of Memento Mori Comments, dailystoic.com/obstacle-is-the-way-summary/.

164 **"Whatever we face, we have a choice"**: Holiday, Ryan. The Obstacle Is the Way: Turning Adversity into Advantage. Penguin Group (USA), 2014.

165 **"You'll have better luck toughening yourself"**: Holiday, Ryan. The Obstacle Is the Way: Turning Adversity into Advantage. Penguin Group (USA), 2014.

167 **subjects who** believed **willpower was unlimited:** Job, Veronika, et al. "Beliefs about willpower determine the impact of glucose on self-control." Proceedings of the National Academy of Sciences(2013): 201313475.

169 **"Once you realize that will power is just"**: "Walter Mischel Quote." A-Z Quotes, www.azquotes.com/quote/719075.

170 **"The brain regulates performance"**: "Train Smarter and Achieve Your Triathlon Goals." Scientific Triathlon, scientifictriathlon.com/tts43/.

171 **still had plenty of muscle available:** Noakes, Tim, and Timothy David OMS. "Fatigue Is a Brain-Derived Emotion That Regulates the Exercise Behavior to Ensure the Protection of Whole Body Homeostasis." Frontiers, Frontiers, 20 Mar. 2012, www.frontiersin.org/articles/10.3389/fphys.2012.00082/full.

171 **"When you think that you are done"**: "David Goggins Quote." AZ Quotes, www.azquotes.com/quote/790296.

172 **Grit is defined as perseverance:** Duckworth, Angela L., et al. "Grit: perseverance and passion for long-term goals." Journal of personality and social psychology 92.6 (2007): 1087.

172 **"There are no shortcuts to excellence":** "Grit Quotes by Angela Duckworth." Goodreads, Goodreads, www. goodreads.com/work/quotes/45670634-grit-passion-perseverance-and-the-science-of-success.

172 **To have grit means that we must remain resilient:** Perkins-Gough, Deborah. "The significance of grit: A conversation with Angela Lee Duckworth." Educational Leadership 71.1 (2013): 14-20.

173 **"You just can't beat the person who never":** "Babe Ruth Quotes." BrainyQuote, Xplore, www.brainyquote.com/ quotes/babe_ruth_379468.

173 **"My goal is to make it so challenging inside":** "#1. When You're a Cleaner... ... You Keep Push Yourself Harder When Everyone Else Has Had Enough." Relentless from Good to Great to Unstoppable, by Tim Grover and Shari Lesser. Wenk, Scribner, 2013, p. 41.

177 **"Hardships often prepare ordinary people":** "'Hardships Often Prepare Ordinary People for an Extraordinary Destiny.'." Passiton.com, www.passiton.com/inspirational-quotes/6940-hardships-often-prepare-ordinary-people-for-an.

CHAPTER 8

180 **The sages gave the king a ring:** Intelligenttree. "Intelligent-Tree." A Poem by Theodre Tilton - This Too Shall Pass Away, 5 Oct. 2007, intelligenttree.blogspot.com/2007/10/poem-by-theodre-tilton-this-too-shall.html.

185 **"the kind of calm equanimity":** Holiday, Ryan. "Achieving Apatheia: 7 Steps To Controlling Your Perceptions Like a Stoic." Medium, Medium, 8 May 2014, medium.com/@Ryan-Holiday/achieving-apatheia-7-steps-to-controlling-your-perceptions-like-a-stoic-14c162be5017.

186 **"Between stimulus and response there is a space":** "A Quote by Viktor E. Frankl." Goodreads, Goodreads, www.

goodreads.com/quotes/8144491-between-stimulus-and-response-there-is-a-space-in-that.

187 **Another Melee player, Justin:** Cameron, Stuart. "Esports Mental Health – Tips for Gamers." Cyber Athletiks, 2018, cyberathletiks.com/esports-mental-health-tips-for-gamers/.

188 **While the neurochemistry and causes of depression:** Nemade, Rashmi, et al. "Biology Of Depression - Neurotransmitters." Mental Help Biology of Depression Neurotransmitters Comments, www.mentalhelp.net/articles/biology-of-depression-neurotransmitters/.

189 **"The concussion didn't heal properly":** McGonigal, Jane. "The Game That Can Give You 10 Extra Years of Life." Ted, Ted, 2012, www.ted.com/talks/jane_mcgonigal_the_game_that_can_give_you_10_extra_years_of_life.

189 **Players complete challenges to help build:** "Superbetter." Games For Change, www.gamesforchange.org/game/superbetter/.

190 **PTG is positive change which helps:** "What Is PTG?" Post-traumatic Growth Research Group, 14 Feb. 2013, ptgi.uncc.edu/what-is-ptg/.

191 **Exercise is better than Zoloft:** "Chapter 5: Depression." Spark: the Revolutionary New Science of Exercise and the Brain, by John J. Ratey and Eric Hagerman, Little, Brown, 2013, pp. 122-123.

191 **The exercises were more likely to stay out:** "Chapter 5: Depression." Spark: the Revolutionary New Science of Exercise and the Brain, by John J. Ratey and Eric Hagerman, Little, Brown, 2013, pp. 135.

191 **"It gets us moving, naturally":** "Introduction." Spark: the Revolutionary New Science of Exercise and the Brain, by John J. Ratey and Eric Hagerman, Little, Brown, 2013, pp. 7.

192 **"Humour remained an important safety":** Cook, Tim. ""I will meet the world with a smile and a joke" Canadian Soldiers' Humour in the Great War." Canadian Military History 22.2 (2013): 5.

194 **"I expected a lot of myself":** Womack, Barrett. "Friendlies: Wobbles; The Man, The Move, The Legend." RedBull.com, 10 Mar. 2015, www.redbull.com/us-en/friendlies-wobbles-the-man-the-move-the-legend.

195 **"I thought, 'I am a disgrace,'":** Global, Panda. "Meet Panda Global: Wobbles the Phoenix." YouTube, YouTube, 21 June 2016, www.youtube.com/watch?v=DaZQFpeIjps.

196 **"When the emotional system becomes overactive":** Tendler, Jared. "What Happens to Your Brain On Tilt?" Mental Game Fish, www.mentalgamefish.com/tilt-poker/.

197 **Overcoming tilt is difficult, but we can regain:** esports, theScore. "What Is Tilt? The Gentle Art of Not Losing Your Sh*t in Esports." YouTube, YouTube, 24 Mar. 2019, www.youtube.com/watch?v=OvaPVBFVUWQ.

200 **"When we increase our heart rate and breathing":** "Chapter 4: Anxiety." Spark: the Revolutionary New Science of Exercise and the Brain, by John J. Ratey and Eric Hagerman, Little, Brown, 2013, pp. 91.

201 **Smiling releases feel-good neurotransmitters:** Riggio, Ronald. "There's Magic in Your Smile." Psychology Today, Sussex Publishers, 25 June 2012, www.psychologytoday.com/us/blog/cutting-edge-leadership/201206/there-s-magic-in-your-smile.

203 **It uses electrical sensors to take in information:** "Biofeedback." Mayo Clinic, Mayo Foundation for Medical Education and Research, 3 Jan. 2018, www.mayoclinic.org/tests-procedures/biofeedback/about/pac-20384664.

203 **Neurofeedback can help us train:** "Neurofeedback." Psychology Today, Sussex Publishers, www.psychologytoday.com/us/therapy-types/neurofeedback.

205 **"We [can] take that data and combine":** Reames, Mitch. "EDGE Wearable Aims to Improve Cognitive Performance in Esports." SportTechie, 2 Aug. 2018, www.sporttechie.com/edge-wearable-aims-to-improve-cognitive-performance-in-esports/.

CHAPTER 9

208 **"As people you are defined by the decisions":** Talks, TEDx. "How to Make Better Decisions | Dr. Joe Arvai | TEDxCalgary." YouTube, YouTube, 8 Dec. 2014, www.youtube.com/watch?v=NQ7SAcFp4so.

209 **Our system 1 thinking is powerful, capable:** Van Rymenant, Marc. "95 Percent of Brain Activity Is beyond Our Conscious Awareness." Neurosciences UX, 1 Aug. 2008, www.simplifyinginterfaces.com/2008/08/01/95-percent-of-brain-activity-is-beyond-our-conscious-awareness/.

209 **Our system 1 thinking is powerful, capable:** Morgan, Nick. "How to Master Yourself, Your Unconscious, and the People Around You -- 3." Forbes, Forbes Magazine, 19 Mar. 2013, www.forbes.com/sites/nickmorgan/2013/03/07/how-to-master-yourself-your-unconscious-and-the-people-around-you-3/#36d6eb636762.

209 **"Our unconscious is really good at quick":** Gladwell, Malcolm. "Blink: The power of thinking without thinking." (2006).

210 **We call this concept thin-slicing:** Silvestre, Dan. "Lessons from Blink: The Power of Thinking Without Thinking by Malcolm Gladwell." Medium, The Startup, 2 Aug. 2018, medium.com/swlh/lessons-from-blink-the-power-of-thinking-without-thinking-by-malcolm-gladwell-ac03aa343eee.

211 **During deliberate decisions:** "Two Distinct Brain Regions Have Independent Influence on Decision-Making." Neuroscience News, Neuroscience News, 1 Sept. 2017, neurosciencenews.com/decision-making-brain-regions-7390/.

211 **"getting off the dance floor":** Linsky, Ronald HeifetzMarty, et al. "A Survival Guide for Leaders." Harvard Business Review, 21 Jan. 2016, hbr.org/2002/06/a-survival-guide-for-leaders.

213 **"We found that a brief period of mindfulness":** "Mindfulness Meditation May Improve Decision-Making, New Study Suggests." ScienceDaily, ScienceDaily, 12 Feb. 2014, www.sciencedaily.com/releases/2014/02/140212112745.htm.

213 **"We found that a brief period of mindfulness":** Hafenbrack, Andrew C., Zoe Kinias, and Sigal G. Barsade. "Debiasing the mind through meditation: Mindfulness and the sunk-cost bias." Psychological Science 25.2 (2014): 369-376.

214 **"Meditation calms down the nerves":** Carpenter, Nicole. "Does Meditation Have a Place in Esports? For Immortals, It

Does." Dot Esports, 13 Aug. 2018, dotesports.com/overwatch/news/immortals-overwatch-team-14177.

215 **There are dozens of biases to be aware of:** "List of Cognitive Biases." Wikipedia, Wikimedia Foundation, 19 Jan. 2019, en.wikipedia.org/wiki/List_of_cognitive_biases.

216 **This is similar to loss aversion":** "Loss Aversion." Behavioraleconomics.com | The BE Hub, www.behavioraleconomics.com/resources/mini-encyclopedia-of-be/loss-aversion/.

217 **"To an outsider, longer thinking":** LoL, Blitz Esports. "How pro LoL Players Move so Fast: the Science behind Gut Reactions in Gaming." YouTube, YouTube, 28 Aug. 2017, www.youtube.com/watch?v=UKAZg__bBlg.

218 **While doing complicated things with their hands:** "Video Games Boost Brain Power, Multitasking Skills." NPR, NPR, 20 Dec. 2010, www.npr.org/templates/transcript/transcript.php?storyId=132077565.

219 **"in a position to make the decision":** Weldon, MindGames. "How to Improve Decision Making in-Game & Get Hyper-Focused ⦿ AskWeldon 88." YouTube, YouTube, 18 Oct. 2016, www.youtube.com/watch?v=G00p6P54Vr8.

221 **players who played Starcraft more often:** Kowalczyk, Natalia, et al. "Real-time strategy video game experience and structural connectivity–A diffusion tensor imaging study." Human Brain Mapping (2018).

221 **"Video game players are able to pick up":** Trudeau, Michelle. "Video Games Boost Brain Power, Multitasking Skills." NPR, NPR, 20 Dec. 2010, www.npr.org/2010/12/20/132077565/video-games-boost-brain-power-multitasking-skills.

221 **games provide an environment where we get:** Raza, Faizan. "Gaming and Self-Development: Why Gaming Helps You Make Better Decisions." Influencive, 17 Sept. 2018, www.influencive.com/gaming-and-self-development-why-gaming-helps-you-make-better-decisions/.

222 **Action video game players developed:** "Video Games Lead to Faster Decisions That Are No Less Accurate." University of Rochester, 13 Sept. 2010, rochester.edu/news/show.php?id=3679.

224 **"The goal of training is to repeatedly"**: Federal Law Enforcement Training Center. Stress and Decision Making. Federal Law Enforcement Training Center, 2011.

CHAPTER 10

231 **"Imagine you are standing in a room"**: Goalcast. "How to Improve Your Focus & Be More Productive | Tom Bilyeu for Goalcast." YouTube, YouTube, 1 July 2018, www.youtube. com/watch?v=HSS-Cr7tzPM.

233 **With too many things to focus on:** Clear, James. "How to Focus Better: Lessons From a Lion Tamer." James Clear, 3 Aug. 2018, jamesclear.com/how-to-focus.

233 **"the cognitive process of selecting"**: "Attention." Science-Daily, ScienceDaily, www.sciencedaily.com/terms/attention. htm.

234 **It is more appropriate to use the term** task switching: "Multitasking." The One Thing: the Surprisingly Simple Truth behind Extraordinary Results, by Gary Keller and Jay Papasan, Bard Press, 2017, p. 45.

235 **Here is a simple strategy you can follow:** Clear, James. "The Ivy Lee Method: The Daily Routine for Peak Productivity." James Clear, 13 July 2018, jamesclear.com/ivy-lee.

236 **"Aristotle once said that"**: Bilyeu, Tom. "Michio Kaku." Impact Theory, 27 Apr. 2018, impacttheory.com/episode/ michio-kaku/.

236 **There are three things we must practice:** Lesyk, Jack. "The Nine Mental Skills of Successful Athletes." Ohio Center for Sport Psychology, www.sportpsych.org/nine-mental-skills-overview.

237 **Even with a minor loss of body weight:** Benton, David. "Memory and Attention Are Affected by Much Lower Levels of Dehydration than Previously Thought." The Conversation, The Conversation, 17 Sept. 2018, theconversation.com/memory-and-attention-are-affected-by-much-lower-levels-of-dehydration-than-previously-thought-63950.

237 **Naps have been shown to:** Rosekind, Mark R., et al. "Crew factors in flight operations 9: Effects of planned cockpit rest

on crew performance and alertness in long-haul operations."
(1994).

237 **Naps have been shown to:** Smith, Simon S., et al. "Napping and nightshift work: effects of a short nap on psychomotor vigilance and subjective sleepiness in health workers." _Sleep and Biological Rhythms_ 5.2 (2007): 117-125.

237 **Naps have been shown to:** Bonnet, M. H. "The effect of varying prophylactic naps on performance, alertness and mood throughout a 52-hour continuous operation." Sleep14.4 (1991): 307-315.

237 **naps were actually the most effective:** Horne, James, Clare Anderson, and Charlotte Platten. "Sleep extension versus nap or coffee, within the context of 'sleep debt'." Journal of sleep research 17.4 (2008): 432-436.

238 **can help improve our cognitive performance:** "The Binaural Power Nap." Own the Day, Own Your Life: Optimized Practices for Waking, Working, Learning, Eating, Training, Playing, Sleeping, and Sex, by Aubrey Marcus, Harper Wave, 2018, pp. 203–2014.

238 **could better control their alpha brain waves:** Trafton, Anne. "The Benefits of Meditation: Neuroscientists Explain Why the Practice Helps Tune out Distractions and Relieve Pain." Medical Xpress - Medical Research Advances and Health News, Medical Xpress, 5 May 2011, medicalxpress.com/news/2011-05-benefits-meditation-neuroscientists-tune-distractions.html.

239 **Meditation also physically changes our brain:** Talks, TEDx. "How Meditation Can Reshape Our Brains: Sara Lazar at TEDxCambridge 2011." YouTube, YouTube, 23 Jan. 2012, www.youtube.com/watch?v=m8rRzTtP7Tc&t=436s.

239 **"I tend to have these blackout moments":** tceliano. "Tiger Zone." YouTube, YouTube, 2 June 2008, www.youtube.com/watch?time_continue=185&v=QEaWvoSBp3A.

240 **"a state in which people are so involved":** "Happiness Revisited." Flow: the Psychology of Optimal Experience, by Mihaly Csikszentmihalyi, Harper Row, 2009, pp. 4.

240 **"Focus gets so intense that everything else disappears":** "Introduction" Stealing Fire: How Silicon Valley, the Navy

SEALs, and Maverick Scientists Are Revolutionizing the Way We Live and Work, by Steven Kotler and Jamie Wheal, Dey St., 2018, p. 4.

241   **"enhances all aspects of physical performance"**: Talks, TEDx. "How to Open up the next Level of Human Performance | Steven Kotler | TEDxABQ." YouTube, YouTube, 2 Dec. 2016, www.youtube.com/watch?v=7xnbUT3rO-vQ&t=585s.

241   **Top executives at consulting firm McKinsey**: Talks, TEDx. "How to Open up the next Level of Human Performance | Steven Kotler | TEDxABQ." YouTube, YouTube, 2 Dec. 2016, www.youtube.com/watch?v=7xnbUT3rOvQ&t=585s.

241   **"you find greater links between that information and"**: Talks, TEDx. "How to Open up the next Level of Human Performance | Steven Kotler | TEDxABQ." YouTube, YouTube, 2 Dec. 2016, www.youtube.com/watch?v=7xnbUT3rO-vQ&t=585s.

242   **found flow could reduce the time it took to train**: Kotler, Steven. "Is The Secret To Ultimate Human Performance The F-Word?" Forbes, Forbes Magazine, 8 Feb. 2014, www.forbes.com/sites/stevenkotler/2014/01/08/the-research-is-in-a-four-letter-word-that-starts-with-f-is-the-real-secret-to-ultimate-human-performance/#35e09629227f.

242   **3 conditions essential for entering flow**: "Enjoyment and the Quality of Life." Flow: the Psychology of Optimal Experience, by Mihaly Csikszentmihalyi, Harper Row, 2009, pp. 48–70.

242   **"Clear goals help [us] identify"**: "Inner Flow." The Rise of Superman: Decoding the Science of Ultimate Human Performance, by Steven Kotler, Quercus, 2015, p. 114.

242   **Cognitive scientist David Simons showed**: TheInvisible Gorilla: And Other Ways Our Intuitions Deceive Us, www.theinvisiblegorilla.com/gorilla_experiment.html.

244   **When our challenge is approximately equal**: "Inner Flow." The Rise of Superman: Decoding the Science of Ultimate Human Performance, by Steven Kotler, Quercus, 2015, p. 116.

245   **Our body flushes hormones out**: Think, Big. "Hack Your Flow: Understanding Flow Cycles, with Steven Kotler." YouTube, YouTube, 15 Oct. 2015, www.youtube.com/watch?v=-JWy_cBcawKQ.

246 **These waves help us bring together disparate thoughts:** "The 5 Brain Waves and Its Connection with Flow State." C Wilson Meloncelli, 12 Nov. 2018, www.cwilsonmeloncelli. com/the-5-brain-waves-and-its-connection-with-flow-state/.

246 **Flow demands a lot from our body:** Think, Big. "Hack Your Flow: Understanding Flow Cycles, with Steven Kotler." YouTube, YouTube, 15 Oct. 2015, www.youtube.com/watch?v=-JWy_cBcawKQ.

246 **Marque Cornblatt, CEO of the Ariel Sports League:** Talks, TEDx. "Flow State: Journey from ICU to Drone Racing Superman | Marque Cornblatt | TEDxHollywood." YouTube, YouTube, 7 Nov. 2016, www.youtube.com/watch?v=FRQkrnc-FaUg.

248 **"Once you have tasted flight":** "A Quote by Leonardo Da Vinci." Goodreads, Goodreads, www.goodreads.com/ quotes/5504-once-you-have-tasted-flight-you-will-forever-walk-the.

CHAPTER 11

250 **The ceramics teacher announced:** Bayles, David, and Ted Orland. Art & Fear: Observations on the Perils (and Rewards) of Artmaking. Image Continuum Press, 1993.

252 **Researchers estimate that it takes on average:** Lally, Phillippa, et al. "How are habits formed: Modelling habit formation in the real world." European journal of social psychology 40.6 (2010): 998-1009.

253 **James Clear outlines four laws of behavior change:** "How to Build Better Habits in 4 Simple Steps." Atomic Habits: Tiny Changes, Remarkable Results: an Easy & Proven Way to Build Good Habits & Break Bad Ones, by James Clear, Random House Busines Books, 2018, p. 54.

253 **James Clear outlines four laws of behavior change:** Clear, James. "The 3 R's of Habit Change: How To Start New Habits That Actually Stick." James Clear, 13 Nov. 2018, jamesclear. com/three-steps-habit-change.

255 **"After a few days you'll have a chain:** Trapani, Gina. "Jerry Seinfeld's Productivity Secret." Lifehacker, Lifehacker.com,

25 June 2013, lifehacker.com/jerry-seinfelds-productivity-se-
cret-281626.

256 **"We don't rise to the level of our expectations"**: "A Quote
by Archilochos." Goodreads, Goodreads, www.goodreads.
com/quotes/387614-we-don-t-rise-to-the-level-of-our-expec-
tations-we.

256 **"Each time you write a page"**: Game, Productivity.
"ATOMIC HABITS by James Clear | Core Message." YouTube,
YouTube, 26 Dec. 2018, www.youtube.com/watch?v=_u8lx-
BrImoc(http://www.youtube.com/watch?v=_u8lxBrImoc).

CHAPTER 12

261 **"Once you know how the mind works"**: Inspired, Be.
"DANDAPANI : How To Control Your Mind (USE THIS to
Brainwash Yourself)." *YouTube*, YouTube, 7 Aug. 2018, www.
youtube.com/watch?v=WYfYmYbp7C4.

APPENDIX

265 **improve memory, improve reaction time:** Examine.com.
"Bacopa Monnieri - Scientific Review on Usage, Dosage, Side
Effects." Examine.com, Examine.com, 9 Oct. 2018, examine.
com/supplements/bacopa-monnieri/.

265 **improve memory, improve reaction time:** Kongkeaw,
Chuenjid, et al. "Meta-analysis of randomized controlled
trials on cognitive effects of Bacopa monnieri extract." Journal of ethnopharmacology 151.1 (2014): 528-535.

266 **attention, language skills, as well as memory:** Kean, James
D., Luke A. Downey, and Con Stough. "A systematic review
of the Ayurvedic medicinal herb Bacopa monnieri in child
and adolescent populations." Complementary therapies in
medicine 29 (2016): 56-62.

266 **improves memory performance:** Vollala, Venkata Ramana,
Subramanya Upadhya, and Satheesha Nayak. "Enhanced
dendritic arborization of hippocampal CA3 neurons by
Bacopa monniera extract treatment in adult rats." Romanian
Journal of Morphology and Embryology 52.3 (2011): 879-886.

266 **boosts antioxidants:** Anbarasi, K., et al. "Effect of bacoside A on brain antioxidant status in cigarette smoke exposed rats." Life Sciences 78.12 (2006): 1378-1384.

266 **inhibit the formation of Beta-amyloid plaques:** Holcomb, Leigh A., et al. "Bacopa monniera extract reduces amyloid levels in PSAPP mice." Journal of Alzheimer's Disease 9.3 (2006): 243-251.

266 **improve blood flow:** Kamkaew, Natakorn, et al. "Bacopa monnieri and its constituents is hypotensive in anaesthetized rats and vasodilator in various artery types." Journal of ethnopharmacology 137.1 (2011): 790-795.

266 **helping reduce anxiety and stress:** Examine.com. "Bacopa Monnieri - Scientific Review on Usage, Dosage, Side Effects." Examine.com, Examine.com, 9 Oct. 2018, examine.com/supplements/bacopa-monnieri/.

266 **helping reduce anxiety and stress:** Benson, Sarah, et al. "An acute, double-blind, placebo-controlled cross-over study of 320 mg and 640 mg doses of Bacopa monnieri (CDRI 08) on multitasking stress reactivity and mood." Phytotherapy research28.4 (2014): 551-559.

266 **helps you feel relaxed and calm:** Examine.com. "L-Theanine: Scientific Review on Benefits, Anxiety, Dosage, Side Effects." Examine.com, Examine.com, 15 Oct. 2018, examine.com/supplements/theanine/

266 **Researchers at Purdue found:** Green, Rodney J., et al. "Common tea formulations modulate in vitro digestive recovery of green tea catechins." Molecular nutrition & food research 51.9 (2007): 1152-1162.

267 **200 mg/200 mg combination of caffeine:** Examine.com. "Caffeine: Proven Health Benefits, Dosage, and More." Examine.com, Examine.com, 29 Mar. 2019, examine.com/supplements/caffeine/.

267 **Choline is used in building and maintaining:** Blalock, Timothy. "Citicoline Vs. Choline." Healthfully, 10 Jan. 2019, healthfully.com/478224-citicoline-vs-choline.html.

267 **benefits primarily in focus:** McGlade, Erin, et al. "Improved attentional performance following citicoline administration in healthy adult women." Food and Nutrition Sciences 3.06 (2012): 769.

267   **and memory:** Alvarez, X. Anton, et al. "Citicoline improves memory performance in elderly subjects." Methods and findings in experimental and clinical pharmacology 19.3 (1997): 201-210.

267   **and memory:** Spiers, Paul A., et al. "Citicoline improves verbal memory in aging." Archives of neurology 53.5 (1996): 441-448.

267   **reduce swelling and blood-brain barrier breakdown:** Başkaya, Mustafa K., et al. "Neuroprotective effects of citicoline on brain edema and blood—brain barrier breakdown after traumatic brain injury." Journal of neurosurgery92.3 (2000): 448-452.

267   **500-2000 mg CDP-choline:** Examine.com. "CDP-Choline: Proven Health Benefits, Dosage, and More." Examine.com, Examine.com, 14 June 2018, examine.com/supplements/cdp-choline/.

267   **300-1200 mg of Alpha GPC:** Examine.com. "Alpha-GPC: Proven Health Benefits, Dosage, and More." Examine.com, Examine.com, 16 Sept. 2018, examine.com/supplements/alpha-gpc/.

267   **attention performance is better at the lower:** Marcus, Lena, et al. "Evaluation of the effects of two doses of alpha glycerylphosphorylcholine on physical and psychomotor performance." Journal of the International Society of Sports Nutrition 14.1 (2017): 39.

267   **build and maintain muscle:** Examine.com. "Creatine Supplement - Unbiased Review on Usage, Dosage, Side Effects." Examine.com, Examine.com, 16 Oct. 2018, examine.com/supplements/creatine/.

267   **improving cognitive processing:** Rawson, Eric S., and Andrew C. Venezia. "Use of creatine in the elderly and evidence for effects on cognitive function in young and old." Amino acids 40.5 (2011): 1349-1362.

268   **improved reasoning and short-term memory:** Avgerinos, Konstantinos I., et al. "Effects of creatine supplementation on cognitive function of healthy individuals: A systematic review of randomized controlled trials." Experimental gerontology (2018).

268   **3-5 g of creatine monohydrate:** "Office of Dietary Sup-
      plements - Dietary Supplements for Exercise and Athletic
      Performance." NIH Office of Dietary Supplements, U.S.
      Department of Health and Human Services, ods.od.nih.gov/
      factsheets/ExerciseAndAthleticPerformance-Consumer/.

268   **improving oxygen flow to your brain:** Hindmarch, I. "Activ-
      ity of Ginkgo biloba extract on short-term memory." Rökan.
      Springer, Berlin, Heidelberg, 1988. 321-326.

268   **120-240 mg:** "Ginkgo Biloba (EGb 761): A Proprietary Leaf
      Extract of Ginkgo Biloba Is Found to Be Safe and Effective
      for Treating Dementia." NursingCenter, www.nursing-
      center.com/journalarticle?article_ID=3168837&Journal_
      ID=54004&Issue_ID=3168438.

268   **120-240 mg:** Examine.com. "Ginkgo Biloba - Scientific
      Review on Usage, Dosage, Side Effects." Examine.com,
      Examine.com, 18 Jan. 2019, examine.com/supplements/gink-
      go-biloba/.

268   **120-240 mg:** Tan, Meng-Shan, et al. "Efficacy and adverse
      effects of ginkgo biloba for cognitive impairment and demen-
      tia: a systematic review and meta-analysis." _Journal of Alz-
      heimer's Disease_43.2 (2015): 589-603.

268   **Goes well with phosphatidylserine:** Examine.com. "Ginkgo
      Biloba - Scientific Review on Usage, Dosage, Side Effects."
      Examine.com, Examine.com, 18 Jan. 2019, examine.com/
      supplements/ginkgo-biloba/.

268   **Goes well with phosphatidylserine:** Kennedy, D. O., et al.
      "Acute cognitive effects of standardised Ginkgo biloba extract
      complexed with phosphatidylserine." Human Psychophar-
      macology: Clinical and Experimental 22.4 (2007): 199-210.

268   **fat-soluble phospholipid commonly found in:** "Phospha-
      tidylserine - Review of Benefits, Effects, Dosage, and More."
      Braintropic, www.braintropic.com/nootropics/phosphati-
      dylserine/.

268   **improve memory:** Kato-Kataoka, Akito, et al. "Soybean-de-
      rived phosphatidylserine improves memory function of the
      elderly Japanese subjects with memory complaints." Journal
      of clinical biochemistry and nutrition 47.3 (2010): 246-255.

268   **reduce stress:** Hellhammer, J., et al. "Effects of soy lecithin phosphatidic acid and phosphatidylserine complex (PAS) on the endocrine and psychological responses to mental stress." Stress 7.2 (2004): 119-126.

268   **300 mg (100 mg taken 3 times daily):** Examine.com. "Phosphatidylserine - Scientific Review on Usage, Dosage, Side Effects." Examine.com, Examine.com, 14 June 2018, examine.com/supplements/phosphatidylserine/.

269   **reducing fatigue:** Ishaque, Sana, et al. "Rhodiola rosea for physical and mental fatigue: a systematic review." BMC complementary and alternative medicine 12.1 (2012): 70.

269   **reducing fatigue:** Qu, Zeqiang, et al. "Pretreatment with Rhodiola rosea extract reduces cognitive impairment induced by intracerebroventricular streptozotocin in rats: implication of anti-oxidative and neuroprotective effects." Biomedical and environmental sciences 22.4 (2009): 318-326.

269   **50-680 mg of rhodiola rosea:** Examine.com. "Rhodiola Rosea: Scientific Review on Usage, Dosage, Side Effects." Examine.com, Examine.com, 30 Sept. 2018, examine.com/supplements/rhodiola-rosea/.

269   **improve memory and concentration:** Awad, Azza S. "Effect of combined treatment with curcumin and candesartan on ischemic brain damage in mice." Journal of Stroke and Cerebrovascular Diseases 20.6 (2011): 541-548.

269   **500 mg curcumin and 20 mg piperine:** Examine.com. "Curcumin - UPDATE 2018 Evidence-Based Review on Benefits, Dosage, Side Effects, & More." Examine.com, Examine.com, 15 Oct. 2018, examine.com/supplements/curcumin/.

270   **improve memory function, and protect your brain:** Saydoff, Joel A., et al. "Oral uridine pro-drug PN401 is neuroprotective in the R6/2 and N171-82Q mouse models of Huntington's disease." Neurobiology of disease 24.3 (2006): 455-465.

270   **improve memory function, and protect your brain:** Teather, Lisa A., and Richard J. Wurtman. "Chronic administration of UMP ameliorates the impairment of hippocampal-dependent memory in impoverished rats." The Journal of nutrition 136.11 (2006): 2834-2837.

270   **improve memory function, and protect your brain:** Koyuncuoglu, Turkan, et al. "Uridine protects against hypoxic-isch-

emic brain injury by reducing histone deacetylase activity in neonatal rats." _Restorative neurology and neuroscience_33.5 (2015): 777-784.

270 **help your brain repair more quickly:** Cansev, Mehmet. "Synaptogenesis: Modulation by availability of membrane phospholipid precursors." Neuromolecular medicine 18.3 (2016): 426-440.

270 **500-1000 mg of uridine:** Examine.com. "Uridine: Proven Health Benefits, Dosage, and More." Examine.com, Examine. com, 14 June 2018, examine.com/supplements/uridine/.

270 **goes well with choline and DHA:** Wurtman, Richard J., et al. "Synaptic proteins and phospholipids are increased in gerbil brain by administering uridine plus docosahexaenoic acid orally." _Brain research_1088.1 (2006): 83-92.

270 **1.3 mg of vitamin B6:** "Office of Dietary Supplements - Vitamin B6." NIH Office of Dietary Supplements, U.S. Department of Health and Human Services, ods.od.nih.gov/ factsheets/VitaminB6-Consumer/.

270 **400 mcg of vitamin B9:** "Office of Dietary Supplements - Folate." NIH Office of Dietary Supplements, U.S. Department of Health and Human Services, ods.od.nih.gov/factsheets/ Folate-Consumer/.

270 **2.4 mcg of vitamin B12:** "Office of Dietary Supplements - Vitamin B12." NIH Office of Dietary Supplements, U.S. Department of Health and Human Services, ods.od.nih.gov/ factsheets/VitaminB12-Consumer/.

271 **1000-2000 IU of vitamin D3:** Examine.com. "Vitamin D: Proven Health Benefits, Dosage, and More." Examine.com, Examine.com, 8 Nov. 2018, examine.com/supplements/vitamin-d/.

271 **Vitamin K is fat soluble with two varieties:** Examine.com. "Vitamin K - Scientific Review on Usage, Dosage, Side Effects." Examine.com, Examine.com, 14 June 2018, examine.com/ supplements/vitamin-k/.

271 **K1 supports blood coagulation, while K2 is more:** Ferland, Guylaine. "Vitamin K, an emerging nutrient in brain function." Biofactors 38.2 (2012): 151-157.

271 **K1 supports blood coagulation, while K2 is more:** Maresz, Katarzyna. "Proper calcium use: vitamin K2 as a promoter of bone and cardiovascular health." Integrative Medicine: A Clinician's Journal 14.1 (2015): 34.

271 **K1 supports blood coagulation, while K2 is more:** Soutif-Veillon, Anne, et al. "Increased dietary vitamin K intake is associated with less severe subjective memory complaint among older adults." Maturitas 93 (2016): 131-136.

271 **90-120 mcg of vitamin K2:** "Office of Dietary Supplements - Vitamin K." NIH Office of Dietary Supplements, U.S. Department of Health and Human Services, ods.od.nih.gov/factsheets/VitaminK-Consumer/.

271 **Adderall actually impaired performance:** Chou, Hsun-Hua, et al. "Amphetamine effects on MATRICS Consensus Cognitive Battery performance in healthy adults." Psychopharmacology227.1 (2013): 165-176.

272 **"Despite the lack of enhancement observed":** Ilieva, Irena, Joseph Boland, and Martha J. Farah. "Objective and subjective cognitive enhancing effects of mixed amphetamine salts in healthy people." Neuropharmacology64 (2013): 496-505.

www.ingramcontent.com/pod-product-compliance
Lightning Source LLC
Chambersburg PA
CBHW071520180526
45171CB00002B/322